The
Upper Division
College

Robert A. Altman

The Upper Division College

Jossey-Bass Inc., Publishers
615 Montgomery Street · San Francisco · 1970

The Jossey-Bass Series in Higher Education

General Editors

JOSEPH AXELROD, *San Francisco State College*

MERVIN B. FREEDMAN, *San Francisco State College and Wright Institute, Berkeley*

Preface

The Upper Division College is a study of the establishment in the United States of those few baccalaureate-granting institutions which admit students only after completion of a minimum of two years of collegiate work and which, themselves, offer the work of only the junior, senior, and in some cases postgraduate years. In a larger sense, however, my book is a history of attempts to modify the four-year baccalaureate degree structure in American higher education, for the establishment of upper division colleges is a direct outgrowth of earlier attempts—such as the Minnesota Plan, the Michigan university system, the Chicago College Plan, and the six-four-four plan—to restructure the "traditional" four-year American baccalaureate.

When my study was begun, seven upper division institutions

were in operation. Since that time, at least eight new colleges have reached various stages of legislative or state board approval, six other states have begun consideration of establishing upper division colleges, and one of the existing institutions has begun adding a freshman and sophomore class. At least one major institution has advocated an experimental professional college to combine the traditional two-year degree of the junior college with the four-year baccalaureate degree in professional areas; a report prepared by four prestigious eastern private secondary schools has suggested creation of a revised edition of the middle school, the equivalent of the virtually extinct four-year junior college.

Throughout the United States, institutions are considering a restructured educational system; as often as not, this restructuring concerns the time sequence of the traditional American baccalaureate as well as the administrative structure of any given institution. And, increasingly, planners are turning to the concept of the upper division institution as the most satisfactory—both politically and educationally—capstone to a growing system of public junior, or community, colleges.

Historically, the American college developed in response to an expanding system of secondary or preparatory education— which increasingly took to itself the basic studies offered in the American college—and to the imported German university ideals, which provided both a methodology and a body of subject matter which the college adopted as its own. Thus, by the middle of the nineteenth century, some American educators began to see the existing four-year college as an anomaly. Rather than offering a unified four-year course of study, the American college appeared to these reformers to combine elements of two divergent systems of education, one of which was the logical conclusion of a student's general, or preparatory, education, while the other was the beginning of professional or research-oriented university work.

Since Germany had been the source of the university concept, many educators turned to Germany for the organizational model on which to base a restructured American system of education. The German system had no college as an intermediate step between preparatory and university work; rather, the "gymnasium" provided all work which was required before entrance to the university, work which was roughly equivalent to that offered through the sophomore year in the American college. As institutions which were called universities developed in the United States during the late nineteenth and early twentieth century, educational leaders such as William Folwell at Minnesota, William Rainey Harper at Chicago, and David Starr Jordan at Stanford suggested that these institutions would not be true universities until they ceased to offer the preparatory, or nonuniversity, courses which then constituted the bulk of their freshman and sophomore offerings.

Building in part on the German model, Harper, Jordan, and others suggested that the logical repository for these basic college offerings was the secondary school system, which should be encouraged to include the thirteenth and fourteenth years. The first junior colleges established in the United States were, in fact, high school departments fostered by Harper's desire to concentrate University of Chicago efforts on the third, fourth, and postgraduate years. In California, Jordan's support contributed greatly to the rapid growth and expansion of junior colleges—many of which began as high school departments. Jordan hoped these institutions would eventually assume the functions of the freshman and sophomore years at Stanford.

Neither Harper nor Jordan succeeded in eliminating the first two years from his institution, although both continued to espouse the separation, or bisection, of the existing American college offerings at the end of the sophomore year. Their theories and support, however, did play a significant role in the development of junior colleges, which, although they did not permit either Chicago or Stanford to eliminate its freshman and sophomore years, eventually provided the base on which new institutions—without the work of the freshman or sophomore years—built. These new institutions, the upper division colleges of the 1950's and 1960's, were not the direct result of educational theories such as those of Harper and Jordan; nonetheless, they were an outgrowth of these theories and of the junior colleges to which the theories had led.

Some of the early upper division institutions, such as the College of the Pacific in Stockton, California, the New School Senior College in New York City, and Concordia Senior College in Fort Wayne, Indiana, were, in fact, a result of educational thinking similar to that of Harper and Jordan; these institutions, however, were developed before the tremendous expansion of junior colleges had been completed following the Second World War. After this expansion, with the work of the first two collegiate years readily available, questions concerning the desirability of splitting the baccalaureate receded in importance. New questions concerning possible ways of offering a baccalaureate education to increasing numbers of students, given the existence of junior colleges, emerged, and with them the development of upper division institutions as a logical capstone to an existing educational system began.

Although some research has been done on the earliest attempts to modify the four-year baccalaureate structure, there has been no research on the origins or development of the postwar upper division institutions and little research concerning other structural modifications in American higher education. Recent books on innovation in education, such as those by Baskin (1965) or Stickler (1964), include little more than footnotes on the upper division experiments, despite chapters on the cluster colleges at the University of the Pacific and on the cooperative education program at Dearborn. Other works, such as that of Knoell and Metzger (1965) —which deals with transfer students in Michigan, among other areas—or Becker (1965)—on the new library system at Florida Atlantic University—never mention that the institution under discussion offers no freshman or sophomore classes. Other works which discuss the conversion of two-year institutions to four-year institutions, such as those of Eells and Martorana (1957a and 1957b), Schultz and Stickler (1965), and Janes (1969), pay little or no attention to the historical context.

Thus, the basic purpose of this study is to document and trace the development of upper division colleges in the larger context of attempts to restructure the traditional American baccalaureate degree. And, in a larger sense, this book is a study of those educators who responded to their immediate needs by creating new structures rather than relying on existing, traditional means of organization. In many instances, the innovation of yesterday has become the tradition of today.

Acknowledgments in a work such as this are always risky to the extent that one to whom thanks are due may be inadvertently omitted. Nonetheless, sincere thanks to E. K. Fretwell, Jr., president of the State University College at Buffalo, for suggesting to me the possibilities in this investigation, and to Michael Brick of Columbia University, for helping me avoid the pitfalls along the way. This study could not have been completed without the financial support of the United States Office of Education, without the cooperation of the presidents of the institutions studied and of their staffs, or without the complete support of my wife, Jane. To all the others—professors, colleagues, and new-found friends—grateful thanks for the assistance without which my book would never have been finished.

Boulder, Colorado   ROBERT A. ALTMAN
March, 1970

Contents

The Upper Division College

The Traditional Baccalaureate

Throughout its development, the American educational system has been shaped by differing definitions of elementary, secondary, and higher education, by differing conceptions of the structure and duration of the institutions at each of these levels, and by differing opinions as to the time required to produce an educated man. The undergraduate college as it is known today, with its four-year baccalaureate degree built upon twelve years of elementary and secondary preparation, is only a relatively recent compromise between the original English collegiate model of the colonial period and the

1

later German university model, which required not only an emphasis on scientific method (which Americans quickly adopted) but also a level of preparation which the American system, in the late nineteenth century, was often unable to offer.

The English college on which Harvard was modeled did not, as is often assumed, offer a four-year course leading to the baccalaureate degree; its program, which usually followed eight years of preparation in a grammar school, was three years in length. Harvard adopted the three-year model but soon found that the preparation provided in the fledgling colonial reading schools, grammar schools, or academies was not adequate for entering college students. To allow for the students' obvious deficiencies, Harvard decided in 1655 to require residence of "three yeares and ten Months at the least" before graduation (cited by Morison, 1936, Vol. 1, p. 80).

As other American colleges were founded before the Revolutionary War, the "traditional" Harvard pattern of four years based on some elementary preparation (primarily a reading knowledge of Greek and Latin) became well established. To a great extent, entrance requirements reflected the studies available to the aspiring student before entering college. Thus, the extension of the grammar schools and the beginnings of the academy movement led Yale, in 1745, to require arithmetic for admission rather than to offer it in the first year.

Yet, the development of public secondary education, as it is known today, was a slow process, especially beyond the Eastern Seaboard. The first public high school was established in Boston in 1821 to serve those not bound for college; the academies retained the function of preparation for further education in conjunction with the colonial grammar schools, which had survived the revolutionary period. However, the subject matter taught in all these institutions was elementary, while the colleges themselves were, at best, teaching subjects which today would be considered appropriate for the secondary school.

Despite the lack of adequate preparatory institutions, colleges in the United States flourished before the Civil War, at least if the incidence of founding is any indication. Donald Tewkesbury (1932, pp. 28, 211–20) lists 182 colleges which were founded before the Civil War and were still operating in 1930; he estimates that these colleges represent at best 20 per cent of those established. By 1870, in only five states, all in the Northeast, were colleges offering preparatory work (Rudolph, 1965, p. 28); a survey by the United States Commissioner of Education the following year showed that approximately 600 communities had graded elementary schools but that the elementary school itself varied from six to ten years in length and was followed by a high school, where one existed, which ranged from one to four years. Where a secondary school existed, colleges were turning over their elementary subjects; in many cases, however, colleges were continuing to expand their own preparatory departments downward to meet the rising elementary schools.

Before 1830, however, the four-year college course remained sacrosanct, at least as a requirement for the Bachelor of Arts degree. Colleges which provided preparatory services did not count this preeducation toward the four years required for the baccalaureate; experimental institutions, such as the Lawrence Scientific School at Harvard and the Sheffield Scientific School at Yale—although offering a degree in three years rather than four—awarded not the Bachelor of Arts but the newly created Bachelor of Science or Bachelor of Philosophy. Other institutions, such as the University of Rochester, the University of Michigan, and the University of North Carolina, also began during the 1850's to experiment with varations of the three-year scientific department, but the degree was always the B.S. or Ph.B.

The first major institution to abandon the four-year requirement for the Bachelor of Arts was Brown University. In 1830, Brown began to allow special students to attend a partial course and, by 1846, had enrolled seventy-two students in the informal series of lectures which composed the course. In 1846, in an attempt to attract more students to the program—a goal which would also motivate the more famous reforms of 1850—the title was changed to the English and scientific course, and outlines were developed for one- and two-year programs of study. At that time, no degree was offered for the scientific course; in 1850, Brown President Francis Wayland recommended extending the course to three years and offering the Ph.B. (Bronson, 1914, pp. 262–269).

In 1850 Wayland (pp. 52–53, 72, 75) proposed far-reaching reforms directed primarily at making higher education more relevant than it had been and motivated, in large measure, by a financial need to increase the number of students. Considering the existing requirements for the Bachelor of Arts degree, Wayland concluded that the only common requirements were "a residence of four years, and the payment of the college bills . . . [since] Degrees are given to candidates of almost every grade of attainment, but never unless the student has made out a given term of residence, and paid the requisite fees." The alternative, "that a degree of A.B. should signify the possession of a certain amount of knowledge, and A.M. of a certain other amount in addition" led Wayland to suggest a master's course of four years, with a baccalaureate of something less, depending upon the subject matter studied.

The experiment at Brown, begun in 1851, barely survived Wayland's retirement four years later. On July 5, 1856, the new president, the Reverend Barnas Sears, in a confidential report not only showed that the number of students entering Brown and the number of students receiving the bachelor's degree were steadily decreasing, even under the new system, but blamed this decrease on the fact that "the character & reputation of the University are injuriously affected by the low standards of scholarship required for the degrees of A.M. & A.B." (cited by Bronson, 1914, p. 321). Accordingly, in September 1857, Brown returned to the requirement of a minimum of four years' residence for the Bachelor of Arts and returned the A.M. to its former status as a degree awarded in course three years after the awarding of the A.B.

Wayland's attempts to modify the structure and duration of the baccalaureate degree were based upon a strong belief that the existing course of study included many subjects which were not of interest or relevance to all students; his reforms were aimed at giving students a greater choice of subjects than they had, decreasing the total requirements for the degree (to bring them into line with existing English requirements, as he saw them), and increasing the attractiveness of a college education at Brown, thus increasing the number of students. Wayland's change in the structure grew out of his concern with the education which his institution would offer and not, as was the case at the University of Michigan, out of an attempt to redefine the relationship of his institution to other institutions within the educational system.

The University of Michigan, founded in 1837 and opened for classes (to six students) in 1841, faced distinctly different problems during the 1850's from those of Brown. Suffering from a lack of strong executive leadership—the presidency was passed annually among the faculty until 1852—and from a situation in which "few towns in the State were able to support more than their primary schools," the University of Michigan grew to eighty-nine students in 1848–1849 (the year in which the preparatory department was closed for lack of students) but fell to fifty-seven students in 1851–1852. The first chancellor, Henry Tappan, was probably correct when, at his inauguration in 1852, he characterized the state primary schools as "poor" and the secondary system as "underdeveloped"; he may have been overly optimistic when he discussed the "so-called University [that] was only an old-fashioned college."[1]

Tappan's major theme, which was to recur with increasing frequency during the next century, was that a university must be a university in more than name. Taking as his model the German educational system, Tappan distinguished between that study which is preparatory (or collegiate) and that which is professional and belongs in a true university. "We are," he stated, "a University faculty giving instruction in a College or Gymnasium. Our first object will be to perfect this gymnasium. . . . We shall thus make our College or Gymnasium an Institution where the youth of our State can freely enter to prepare themselves for professional study" (cited by Cowley, 1942, p. 199).

Yet, Tappan did not propose, as President William Watts Folwell of the University of Minnesota was to do seventeen years later, that the University of Michigan rid itself of its nonuniversity function. "Our first object," he said, "will be to perfect this gym-

[1] Factual material concerning the University of Michigan is drawn from Farrand (1885) and Hinsdale (1906).

nasium. To this end we propose a scientific course parallel to the classical course." And, unlike the three-year scientific courses at the Lawrence and Sheffield schools, "the entire [scientific] course will run through four years. . . . Students who pursue the full scientific course we shall graduate as Bachelors of Science" (cited by Hinsdale, 1906, p. 44).

The key point in Tappan's proposals, in terms of the structure and duration of the collegiate experience, was the equating of the entire college with the gymnasium, both of which were seen as preliminary to a true university experience. Burke A. Hinsdale, reflecting more the thinking of his own times than that of Tappan's, saw that "his [Tappan's] University ideal involved the transference of the teaching done in this College to secondary or gymnasial schools" (1906, p. 43). Yet, although Hinsdale assumed, as many educators were to do in the future (Eells, 1936; Cowley, 1942), that preparatory work does not belong in a university, he also saw the college as a combination of preparatory and professional studies, some of which could rightly remain within a university while others should be relegated to the preparatory, or gymnasial, schools. To Tappan, however, whose institution contained no professional studies in 1852 and had only five years earlier felt the need to set a minimum entry age at fourteen, this split within the college was neither real nor perceived; his college *was* a preparatory, or gymnasial, school.

Following the Civil War, when the elective system and specialized professional courses modeled on the German universities had become more widespread than they had been before in American higher education, a true distinction between preparatory and university education developed in many American colleges. In the 1850's, however, when Tappan first proposed that the college itself was a gymnasium and that this structure must be perfected before the University of Michigan could get on to the more important business of being a university, this distinction was not yet valid for most American institutions.[2]

[2] Frederick Eby (1932, p. 471) states that "the point of supreme significance for those who wish to understand the situation [the development of the four-year junior college in Eby's mind, but equally apt in the current

While Tappan was concerned with the perfection of the college, officials at the University of Georgia (then known as Franklin College) were concerned with the mere survival of their institution. Enrollment at the "small classical college" was falling steadily and, in 1855, reached 182, its lowest in ten years. (During the same period, under Tappan, enrollment at Michigan was rising rapidly and would reach 850 by 1863, the year of Tappan's sudden, forced departure.) An economic depression, reflected in and worsened by consistent action by the Georgia legislature to cut the college budget, had also limited the number of students who could afford to attend. In addition, competition from private and denominational colleges—fifty new colleges were established in Georgia between 1835 and 1861, although only six of them survived (Tewkesbury, 1932, pp. 28, 175)—was draining the already dwindling source of potential students.[3]

Moreover, severe dissension existed within the college. Several of the younger teachers, disturbed by the youth and immaturity of the students and their own inability to introduce new subjects, such as geology, were in open rebellion against the president, "Dr. [Alonzo] Church, conservative and wise, [who] opposed radical changes being made and declared that the university system was unsuited to the age at which students attended this college." The young teachers, on the other hand, "were contending for a real University, using university methods and management to supplant the outworn detention station called Franklin College." The result, in October 1856, when enrollment had dropped to seventy-nine students, was the firing of all professors and the president; only the president and those with whom he agreed were rehired.

The Board of Trustees was under the most pressure, caught, on the one hand, between the president and his staff and, on the other, between mounting costs and dwindling state support. The

---

discussion] was the upward evolution of the traditional college of a century ago. At the beginning it was a typical four-year secondary school in methods of instruction, curriculum, organization, and atmosphere. . . . In its development upward, it added two years of time, but these two years were university in character. Since the change the four-year college has not been a unity."

[3] Factual material concerning the University of Georgia is drawn from Brooks (1956), Coulter (1928), and Hull (1894).

board had suggested, in November 1855, a reorganization plan to create four new affiliated schools and to draw increased support from the legislature; this plan had been killed by the Georgia senate, which, in view of the obvious internal difficulties of the institution and the worsening economic situation, cut off all financial support. The board was experiencing difficulty in replacing those professors who had left the school in protest against Church's administration (or who had been fired during the 1856 revolt), and it now changed its position vis-à-vis Church. With enrollments continuing to fall well below the level (100 students) necessary to operate without state support and under new pressures from the trustees, Church resigned in November 1858, effective at the close of that academic year.

The board, convinced that the institution could be saved only through change and that "the institution could be changed only by a radical reorganization," moved quickly. In May 1859, before Church had vacated his office, a "Programme of an Enlarged Organization of the University of Georgia" was published; it identitfied the major problem as the students' youth and proposed linking the preparatory division (the Academy) with the first two years of collegiate study so that students could "be watched over night and day, till fully prepared for the Junior Class." On August 4, 1859, the trustees formally created a Collegiate Institute to perform this function and, on November 3, 1859, announced that "the University of Georgia shall consist of a Collegiate Institution, a College Proper [which would include only the junior and senior years], and University Schools of Science and Philosophy." The existing institution was closed, and a search was begun for a new chancellor (as he was to be called) and staff.

By September 1860, the trustees had assembled a chancellor, the Reverend Andrew A. Lipscomb, and a staff of five professors with which to open the new College Proper; at the same time, they secured a promise of funds from the state and began a fundraising campaign for the new buildings to house the Collegiate Institute (the old Academy combined with the former freshman and sophomore years). From that point, however, and through no fault of any concerned with the university, events led steadily downhill until the institution, on February 4, 1864, was once again forced to close its doors. When it reopened on January 5, 1866, the high school was again separate, and the brief experiment was at an end.

Without question, the primary cause of the failure was the outbreak of war. Having opened in January 1861 with 120 juniors and seniors, the university soon lost seventy-five students who enlisted following the secession of Georgia. Enrollment continued to decline, and following a complete mobilization after the fall of Chattanooga, only twenty students remained in the College Proper. At Lipscomb's recommendation, as a final effort to save the College Proper, the freshman and sophomore years were once again added on July 4, 1863; the total registration, by January 1, 1864, had risen to forty students. It was, however, not enough, and the university was closed "for the duration" in early February 1864. The first upper division institution had lasted a total of thirty months, and seven months later, the entire university was closed.

Although most scholars interested in the bisection of the college agree that the University of Georgia was the first operating institution to "successfully" eliminate its own freshman and sophomore years, they make little or no attempt to see these events as anything more than a historical oddity (Cowley, 1942, p. 193; Eells, 1936, p. 136; Smart, 1967, p. 13); they were a precursor, perhaps, but only indirectly since the University of Georgia is not considered to be in the mainstream of American educational thought, nor is Lipscomb regarded as a great educational innovator. Scholars usually note the University of Georgia as a first and continue the discussion of Tappan, Folwell, or William R. Harper—men who, it is assumed, were more conscious of the significance of their own educational thinking.

Yet, in many ways, the University of Georgia was typical of American colleges immediately before the Civil War; what was atypical was the response the institution made to its problems. Its students were young—too young to suit some of the faculty—and one may assume that the level of instruction was correspondingly low. Yet, whereas the University of Michigan legislated a minimum age for entrance, Georgia responded by keeping the younger students within the university but in a separate school. This decision was facilitated since Franklin College had (and needed—and had no desire, even after its reorganization, to relinquish) its own preparatory division, a common occurrence among institutions outside the Northeast. Thus, Georgia eliminated the younger students by cutting two years from the College Proper and by designating them as preparatory to formal college work.

Of perhaps greater significance, the problems at Georgia were typical of those associated with the first inroads of science, which would be felt in most institutions after, rather than before, the Civil War. The younger teachers wanted certain sciences; Church felt that they had no place in an institution serving such young students. At heart, however, was a question not so much of age but of the subjects to be taught. Although few at the University of Georgia articulated the distinction between the gymnasial (preparatory) and university (professional) studies, the distinction was, nonetheless, central to the dispute between Church and those who left the institution before him.

Finally, the institution was typical in its enrollment and financial difficulties. Many institutions faced and weathered the challenge of denominational colleges, but the University of Georgia, located not in Atlanta but in rural Athens, suffered from its own internal strife and from the mistrust of the distant legislature, on which it depended greatly for its support. After the Civil War, under the aegis of the Morrill Act, the university was literally reborn; in the 1850's, it sought a solution to its financial crises by concentrating its spending only on the last two years.

Robert P. Brooks (1956, pp. 38–42) implies that the Academy, to which the freshman and sophomore years were joined, was supported independently of the college, although no specific discussion of such support appears in any of the works on this period of the history of the university. One may assume, however, that the Academy did not face the same competition as did the university from the denominational colleges; in fact, if one assumes the same lack of preparatory education in Georgia as was evident throughout the rest of the country, it was probably doing well. One should note that when the Collegiate Institute was opened in its new organization on January 1, 1862, it had already raised enough money to finance three buildings. As of July 1, 1863, the College Institute enrolled five times as many students as did the College Proper, although part of this difference is probably due to the young age of the College Institute students, which made them less eligible for military service. The enrollment of 120 students in the College Proper at its opening in 1861 testifies, in part, however, to what might have been a successful experiment had it not been for the outbreak of war. For some reasons—and these, interestingly enough, are never specified—students enrolled in greater numbers in the new institution than they had in the old, which contained two additional years. Where the students came from and why remain questions for further study.

By 1866, when the University of Georgia was reopened, the new organizational pattern was dead. Adopted more for expediency and enrollment than for educational or philosophical considerations, the pattern of the Collegiate Institute and the College Proper was now, following passage of the Morrill Act and the influx of students returning from the war, discarded. Yet, the basic issues which had arisen during the controversies of the 1850's—the role of science in the curriculum, the proper age for university studies, and the relationship between the preparatory and the new professional courses—appeared repeatedly in differing forms during the next three decades as American higher education entered the age of the university.

The next institution to become concerned with these questions as they related to the organization and duration of the college program was the University of Minnesota; under the dynamic leadership and educational thought of its new president, Folwell, Minnesota was the first American institution to combine a philosophical concern for the role of the university with specific organizational reforms aimed at bisecting the American college.

Speaking at his inauguration in 1869, Folwell sounded a theme similar to that of Tappan seventeen years earlier: The college, as it then existed, was nothing more than a preparatory or secondary school. Folwell's ultimate goal was "a three-fold scheme of education. 1st, The common schools. 2nd, The colleges or secondary schools. 3rd, The university." In order to achieve this goal,

Folwell saw some older and richer institutions (including, one must assume, the eighteen-year-old University of Minnesota) assuming "the university character," while "the greater number, without doubt, will be forced to return to their original and natural position as secondary schools" (Folwell, 1909, p. 35).

Folwell's concept of this university character is important, for it shows clearly the influence of the German educational system on his thinking. To Folwell, an institution which was "a federation of schools . . . embracing potentially all subjects of human and practical interest; teaching always with reference to principles; occupying ever an attitude of investigation; knowing no favorite studies; at all times thoroughly involved with the scientific spirit; that is the University." Preceding the university in Folwell's educational system were the secondary schools or colleges (with little or no distinction between them) taking the place of the gymnasium, which preceded the university in his German model. Folwell rejoiced at the gain to be achieved "as soon as we should be able to relegate to these schools [public secondary schools and private denominational colleges] those studies which now form the body of work for the first two years in our ordinary American colleges."

Folwell (pp. 36–37) writes, in an author's note, that "away back in the '50's when the speaker was a schoolboy, he enjoyed the friendship of Professor Charles A. Joy of Columbia College, who had taken up his life work after a long period of study in German universities. From him came the knowledge of the gymnasium, the splendid secondary school, fitting German boys for the work of men in the university. During nearly twenty years of teaching, military service and business the idea incubated. With great trepidation the speaker ventured on this (for him) most important occasion [his inauguration in 1869] to announce the principle of a system of public instruction with its natural trinity of epochs, primary, secondary, superior."

Thus, where Tappan had proposed to perfect the gymnasial, or secondary, schools within the university, Folwell proposed that the universities rid themselves of this function. Colleges (or secondary schools) should provide, according to Folwell, "all those studies which as a boy he [the student] ought to study, 'under tutors and governors.' Then let the boy, grown up to be a man, emigrate to the university, to be master of his time and studies, to enjoy perfect 'academic freedom,' keeping only to the rule, of so using his own as not to harm another." Yet, this plan required an American counterpart to the German gymnasium when there were not even institutions capable of preparing students to enter the college as it then existed. "There were not, in 1871, six schools, public or private, in the whole state," Folwell lamented in 1875, "fitting students to enter college" (pp. 37–38, 100).

Folwell's response was to establish "a department of secondary instruction of wider range than customary . . . [which] will be found to correspond in *location,* in *object,* and in *scope,* with the gymnasia and real schools of Germany and the lyceums of France and Switzerland." Into this Department of Elementary Instruction, created in 1872, went the work of the old preparatory department (begun in 1867) and that of the existing freshman and sophomore years. Following completion of this program of study, the student would "graduate" to the university studies of the junior and senior years (pp. 100–101, 103).

Regardless of Folwell's theories, as enunciated in his inaugural address and later speeches, in reality the student would at no time be outside the University of Minnesota during his studies, whether preparatory or university. Although Folwell went further than did Tappan in suggesting that the traditional studies of the first two years of college "belong, of their nature, to the secondary period, and to that place our Minnesota plan relegates them" (pp. 102–103), Folwell's ultimate result was similar to that at Michigan: to bring the first two collegiate years and the old preparatory studies into the university more firmly than ever.

Many prominent educators supported Folwell's Minnesota Plan, first outlined in a speech at the 1875 meeting of the National Education Association, although most read into it and approved that which was of greatest concern to their own institutions. From the University of Michigan, President James B. Angell wrote supporting attempts at reform which "carried secondary education up to the mark you have set"; in 1883, Michigan instituted its own university system, which provided for a lower division to offer general education and an upper division, in which students pursued a well-defined course within their own major. From Harvard, where a rapidly expanding elective system and concern with the advancing age of college graduates soon led to proposals for shortening the baccalaureate course, the Reverend A. P. Peabody wrote that "you have placed the elective system just where it ought to stand." President Read (University of Missouri) congratulated Folwell on "the correct view of agricultural education," while President Andrew White, fresh from his own innovations at Cornell, called the Minnesota Plan an excellent idea "in view of the peculiarities of your immediate education in the state" (cited by Folwell, 1909, pp. 135–141).

Folwell did not succeed in removing preparatory work from the university, nor did his plan to formally split the college into its preparatory and university components endure past his retirement from Minnesota in 1884. The problem of defining the role of the newly developing universities, as well as their structure, duration, and relationship to the rest of American education, continued throughout the nineteenth century as other educators attempted solutions, some similar to Folwell's and others based on a different conception of university education. The theoretical base for much of the future discussion had been laid; a respected educator had questioned the solid four-year structure of the baccalaureate degree in both thought and action.

By the mid-1880's, several trends in the American adaptation of German university ideals had become apparent. The basic college curriculum was changing, as science and the elective system forced continuing expansion of the traditional liberal arts offerings. At the graduate level, the German ideal of the scientific method became enshrined. Concurrently, the growth of professional schools within the developing universities led to questions concerning the appropriate preparation for admission to graduate study; some educators even suggested that the baccalaureate degree be demanded of those who would study law or medicine. The American university became, as Folwell had desired, a federation of schools, but the four-year English residential college remained the hub around which the new schools were organized. The concept of the university was thus confused. On the one hand, it represented a method of inquiry which was drawn, to a great extent, from the German universities. On the other hand, it was ultimately to be an organizational structure which differed distinctly from the German model, which dominated the thinking of many educators. The failure of some educators to separate the German methodology from the German model was a primary source of the resulting difference of opinion as to how the new American university should be structured.

Attempts to modify the four-year baccalaureate curriculum after the Civil War developed along two lines, each conditioned by a desire to have the American system conform to the German system, from which the basic concepts of graduate education were being borrowed. Angell of Michigan stated both approaches in 1890: "If we were organizing anew a system of education in the west, we should doubtless construct one differing in many particulars from the present. We should be likely to establish *secondary schools resembling the German gymnasium,* and do in them the work now accomplished in the first year of college, perhaps even that of the second year. *The University might then complete its work,* as the German university does, *in three years."* What separated Angell from other would-be reformers was his initial condition. Recognizing that he was not organizing a system anew, he concluded that "at present it seems best for us to continue our present policy by which students generally continue their work three and a half or four years in the collegiate course" (pp. 16–17, italics mine).

Other educators, however, disagreed, not with the possible changes which Angell had outlined but with his conclusion that the best present policy was continuation of the past. White of Cornell called for colleges "to begin their freshman year two years earlier than the present freshman year. . . . After its four years' work let the college bestow its diplomas or certificates upon its graduating classes, and then let those who desire it be admitted into the universities" (cited by Cowley, 1942, pp. 201–202). White's proposal, which sounds distinctly like the six-four-four plan of school organization in the 1930's, was predicated upon the assumptions that the universities were distinct from the colleges and that colleges could do preparatory work better by starting and finishing earlier than was presently the case.

Nicholas Murray Butler agreed with White. As early as 1892, Butler (cited by Cowley, 1942, p. 204) wrote that "the college can begin its work earlier. . . . It can retain its four years' course, and yet yield its students to the university at eighteen or nineteen." By 1901, Butler, then president of Columbia, remained concerned for the age at which students graduated from college, but his proposals had been slightly modified. His concern with age was now tied to the debate regarding requirements for admission to graduate work. "While I hold a secondary school education to be too low a standard for admission to professional study at Columbia University," Butler (1902) wrote, "personally I am of the opinion that to insist upon graduation from the usual four-years' college course is too high a standard to insist upon." Butler's proposal was to develop a two-year collegiate course (which he saw as equivalent to the French baccalaureate and to that required for an American baccalaureate in 1860) for those wishing to continue into the professional schools, while offering a four-year master's degree for those desiring only the liberal arts. To Butler, a three-year course "for all students [then being debated at Harvard and elsewhere] involves an unnecessary sacrifice."

Butler's views were, according to W. H. Cowley, contradicted by an earlier statement that "to confuse the American college with the German university is inexcusable. . . . An educational organization closely following the German type would not meet our needs so well as the yet unsystematic, but remarkably effective, organization that circumstances have brought into existence" (cited by Cowley, 1942, p. 204). Yet, Butler had never proposed that the gymnasial model be followed in the United States. The confusion is Cowley's, who discusses Butler's proposals under the general heading "Efforts to Divide the College in Half" (including attempts at Michigan, Minnesota, Cornell, and Columbia) as opposed to "Efforts to Reduce the College to Three Years." Actually, there is a greater distinction between Folwell and Butler than between Butler and Eliot; Folwell, in a situation where secondary or preparatory instruction was inadequate, was concerned with providing preparatory work and used the gymnasium as his model. Butler, concerned with the age of college graduates and with the total length of secondary, collegiate, and university studies (each section being distinct from the others), proposed a shorter baccalaureate as a means of lowering the age of college graduates.

Butler and White were not alone in their concern for the length of the existing baccalaureate course and the age at which students were being prepared to enter professional studies. Butler's predecessor at Columbia, President F. A. P. Barnard (1886, pp. 22–24, 31), had opened the debate on that campus by arguing for elective courses for those past nineteen years of age; since the body matures at nineteen, said Barnard, one must assume that the brain does also and act accordingly. In essence, Barnard was thus arguing for two distinct programs within Columbia College, the prescribed (preparatory) and the elective (professional). At Cornell, President Charles Kendall Adams (1890, pp. 20–22) presented his trustees with a detailed study of the proposals under discussion by Barnard (at Columbia) and Eliot (at Harvard); Adams expressed no opinion in his report but warned the trustees that the movement to modify the baccalaureate degree was gaining ground and that Cornell would soon be required to make decisions of its own.

The evil which these prominent educators sought to prevent was clear, at least on the East Coast, where public and private secondary schools were now providing a lengthening program of studies before college. Whereas in the Midwest the debate centered around the role of the college as a preparatory school for university studies, in the East the colleges were no longer offering any significant amount of preparatory (high school or gymnasial) work. Folwell saw a threefold scheme of education (elementary, college or secondary, and university), but Daniel Coit Gilman (1891, pp. 3, 5), president of Johns Hopkins, saw three scholastic periods corresponding to the school (for what was essential), the college (for what was liberal), and the university (for what was special or professional). The increasing number of students completing the combined high school-college education at ages approaching twenty-one and twenty-two, coupled with the move to require a degree for entry into the professional schools, was leading to a situation in which "those who pursue a collegiate and then a professional course post-pone, till too late a period, the actual business of life."

The leader of the movement to shorten the baccalaureate work in order to allow for earlier graduation and advancement to the professional schools was unquestionably Eliot of Harvard. As early as 1885, Eliot (1886, p. 14) commented on the "unreasonable postponement of entrance into practice" of professional school graduates and proposed a plan for "the abridgement of the College course by those students who go from College directly into one of the professional schools of the University." A year later, Eliot (1887, p. 16) reported upon another proposal to shorten the college course: "that the First Year studies of the Medical School be counted also, under certain conditions, for the degree of A.B."

The issue was perhaps most clearly put by Dean Clement L. Smith, one of Eliot's most trusted lieutenants. "The standard of our Bachelor's degree," wrote Smith, "was pushed forward to its present advanced position at a time when that degree marked the limit of liberal study for all but an inconsiderable number of students." The development of the Harvard elective system, however, had enabled the university to offer courses in many fields "sufficient for a course extending far beyond the traditional four years. . . . The full course of liberal study, which will be pursued by the smaller number, must therefore be divided into parts, of which one corresponds to the present college course, while the other is designed for special study, leading to a higher degree." This division would not, however, occur at the end of the existing four-year course; "the point at which the student may profitably begin to devote himself to the pursuit of special study" would probably be "reached at least by the end of the present Junior year" (cited by Eliot, 1887, pp. 75–76).

The issue was debated at Harvard over several years. On November 16, 1887, the Academic Council voted "that with a view to lower the average age at which Bachelors of Arts of Harvard College can enter the professional schools and the Graduate Department, the College Faculty be requested to consider the expediency of a reduction of the College course" (cited by Eliot, 1888, pp. 12–13). The faculty did consider the matter but did not arrive at a decision until March 26, 1890; even then, the four-point compromise, defining the degree in terms of courses of study completed instead of in terms of time, was passed by the relatively narrow margin of thirty-four to twenty-two. At hearings conducted by the Board of Overseers, six additional negative votes were recorded (from three new faculty members and three not voting), raising the minority strength to twenty-eight out of sixty-two. Finally, on April 8, 1891, the board rejected three of the four proposals, effectively killing the attempt at reform. "Measures on this subject," Eliot (1891, pp. 7–9) reported, "must commend themselves to the judgment of a large majority of the teachers of the University, before they can be accepted by the Board of Overseers." Sadly, for Eliot, his reform proposals had not.

Eliot and his supporters did not give up. At the 1903 convention of the National Education Association, Eliot (1903, pp. 496, 498) noted that "the period devoted to professional education has been more than doubled within the last forty years in the United States" and that Harvard, which now required the A.B. for admission to all its graduate schools and departments except divinity, was pushing toward a plan to shorten the baccalaureate program, although still requiring candidates "to pass exactly the same number of examinations on the same number of courses as are required of the man who takes the degree in four years." Others, such as Andrew West (1903), dean of the Princeton Graduate School, were now advocating Eliot's earlier proposals to combine elements of the junior and senior years with graduate study for those who wanted to continue their studies past the baccalaureate.

Yet, the traditional four-year baccalaureate in the established eastern schools, having successfully withstood the challenge from Eliot's proposals at prestigious Harvard, now appeared secure, and voices in opposition to Eliot's ideas were raised with increasing frequency. "The American public is not crying for *young* men," wrote Professor Thomas Seymour (1897, p. 714) of Yale. "Compared with half a century ago our people have a distinct distrust for young men. The demand of the day is for *well-trained* men of broad views." "The college unit stands for an idea, guaranteed by a degree," argued President William J. Tucker (1897, p. 696) of

Dartmouth, "and is, therefore, entitled to sufficient time to make good the demands which fall upon it."

Although the debate continued on the East Coast for several more years and two institutions, Johns Hopkins (1876–1907) and Clark University (1902–1922), offered the three-year baccalaureate degree, the tradition of the four-year college built upon a solid secondary background had won the day. In the Midwest, however, where the line between secondary and higher education was less well defined, new answers were being found to old questions regarding the duration and scope of a college education. In 1904, Edmund J. James, the new president of the University of Illinois, repeated his call for admission to graduate school after two years of college, a proposal originally offered during James's tenure as president of Northwestern University and based upon his experience at the Wharton School of the University of Pennsylvania, where students were admitted after two years of liberal arts preparation at the college (James, 1891, p. 20). And, in 1892, an institution opened in Chicago which specialized, for the next sixty years, in finding new ways to organize and divide the baccalaureate experience.

Two

~~~~~~

Bisection of the Baccalaureate

~~~~~~

The University of Chicago was opened on October 1, 1892, eighteen months after the Board of Overseers had killed Charles W. Eliot's proposals to shorten the baccalaureate program at Harvard and eight years after the end of William W. Folwell's Minnesota Plan. As in the great majority of American colleges and universities, the degree to be offered at Chicago was a four-year baccalaureate in arts, science, or philosophy; yet, the internal organization of the institution, its relationships to other educational institutions, and the educational philosophy of its designer and first president,

21

William Rainey Harper, had profound effects on the structure of the baccalaureate program in American higher education.

Harper (1903, p. 505) believed, as had Henry Tappan and Folwell before him, that there was a distinction between work "of the same scope of character as that of the preceding years in the academy or high school" and "the real university work done in the junior and senior years" of college. His ultimate solution was a combination of that proposed by Tappan—that the role of the university was first to perfect that preparatory work which it, of necessity, offered—and that proposed by Folwell—that the university could not play its proper role until preparatory work was eliminated from it entirely. Harper created an institution in which the work of the first two years (preparatory) was clearly distinct from that of the last two years (university) and which, through its program of affiliations, would eventually "devote its energies mainly to the University Colleges and to strictly University work" (cited by Storr, 1966, p. 117).

The University of Chicago had five major divisions: university extension, university press, university libraries, university affiliations, and the university proper. The first three divisions—extension, press, and libraries—"were common, in one form or another, to all universities"; Harper's hopes and plans for bringing order into the educational system of the day were embodied in the university proper and the university affiliations (Goodspeed, 1925, p. 54). The ideas for both were not new to American education, although the specific purposes and uses of both plans were unique to Harper's Chicago.

The university proper—the branch which was to provide instruction on campus for credit—was composed of the Colleges of Arts, Literature and Science, "each of the colleges with respect to its work being divided into a University College and an Academic College." The academic college offered "the lower half of the curriculum, ordinarily known as the work of the Freshman and Sophomore classes," while the university college offered "the upper half of the curriculum, ordinarily known as the work of the Junior and Senior classes." Students who completed the work of the academic college, whether at Chicago or at one of its affiliated institutions, were "graduated therefrom and given a certificate of admission to the University College," in which they would complete the required work for the baccalaureate degree (University of Chicago, 1895, p. 11).

By 1898, the names of the colleges within the university proper had been changed from academic and university to junior and senior, and the catalogue description had become more generalized. In 1895, the catalogue stated that work ordinarily done in the first two years was to be "designated Academic College"; by 1898, the catalogue declared that "the first half of the curriculum in a college, ordinarily known as the work of the Freshman and Sophomore years, constitutes the work of a Junior College" (University of Chicago, 1898, pp. 7–8, 9). The requirements for admission to the junior college remained the same as those for admission to the academic college, but Harper had gone beyond designating names for colleges within his university and was now defining what constituted a new institution in American higher education, the junior college. According to Walter C. Eells (1931, p. 47), "as far as known this is the first use of the term 'junior college,' although it was not until a few years later that it was used, also by President Harper, to designate an institution entirely distinct from the university."

Closely tied to Harper's concept of a bisected baccalaureate program (which is what his junior and senior college plan amounted to) was the use of affiliation and cooperation contracts with high schools and colleges. Affiliated secondary institutions became, in the strictest sense, departments of the university through university representation on the local board of control and university participation in appointments, examinations, and certification of completion. At the same time, qualified institutions were encouraged to continue their offerings through the first two years of college, as was begun at Joliet, Illinois, in 1902. The result, Harper hoped, would be "the growth and development of high school and the probability that this growth will not stop until two years of college work have been added to the present curriculum of the high school," which would permit "the higher work [to] be given all out strength on the campus" (cited by Goodspeed, 1916, p. 247).

Harper's plans for affiliated colleges were less successful than those for affiliated high schools, probably because the colleges were asked to give up a major part of their function while the high schools were encouraged to add to their present offerings. At the outset, affiliated colleges were "to adopt so far as may be practicable the courses of study and the general regulations of the Colleges of the University of Chicago," to share control of hiring and firing with the university, and "to employ only the University Examinations in all subjects taught in The College" (cited by Storr, 1966, pp. 212–213). Despite the promise of the university to furnish assistance in purchasing and to grant diplomas and credit to the students of the affiliated colleges on a par with those offered to students in the university academic colleges, the idea never caught on, partially out of fear of "academic imperialism" and partially because of Harper's suggestion that a majority of weaker colleges should eventually eliminate their upper divisions and offer the work of only the first two years.

Although Harper was not in favor of retaining many of the weaker small colleges (he estimated that about 25 per cent of the small colleges should and would survive), he was not against small institutions per se. "The existence of the smaller colleges is not only a desirable thing," he wrote in 1902 (pp. lxvi–lxvii), "it is a necessity in the intellectual growth of the great sections of the country which make up the West, the Northwest and the South." Furthermore, Harper did not suggest that the other 75 per cent of the small colleges should perish; on the contrary, he wanted some of them to become junior colleges in order to concentrate their resources on that portion of the educational program which they could best provide. Harper jokingly stated that if his plans were successful, the University of Chicago might change "from an institution which gives a course of training and cultivation to an institution which estmates the work of various smaller institutions and confers degrees." Given the fear of the small colleges of being absorbed or reduced to insignificance, Harper's concern was groundless.

By 1904, six affiliated high schools in five states had developed elongated programs which included two years of junior college work; by the same time, no institutions of higher education (with the exception of some small Baptist colleges in Texas and Missouri) had offered to eliminate their last two years in order to affiliate with the University of Chicago. Four other high schools or academies were affiliated with the university, and six colleges (three of them Baptist)[1] had signed affiliation agreements, although none had voluntarily offered to reduce its offerings.

Harper's belief in the divisibility of the college course—and of the virtue in such a move—did not die with him in 1906, although his plan for extensive affiliations which would provide the first two years of collegiate work was never fully realized. The essential division between the junior and senior colleges at Chicago remained virtually unchanged until the creation of the Chicago College Plan in 1930, which widened rather than narrowed the split between the two halves of the baccalaureate program. Despite growing alarm on the part of many educators that the college itself was threatened by Harper's plans and despite the support that the plan continued to receive from Harper's successors at the university, no major modifications of Harper's designs were made during the quarter century following his death. Harper's successor, Harry Pratt Judson, wrote in 1915 that "the Junior Colleges cover work which could be done and should be done in the secondary schools . . . and the likelihood of being able to slough off this Junior College work . . . seems stronger today than it ever has been since the University opened" (cited by Goodspeed, 1916, pp. 154–55).

Harper did not foresee the end of the four-year college, as some feared. His ultimate goal—to bring order to the developing educational structure he faced in the Midwest—required that some students receive a general education through secondary school and junior colleges (which might also be part of the secondary system) before entering a university for specialized study, while others receive an extended liberal education in those four-year colleges which

[1] The significance of the affiliating colleges' being Baptist lies in the fact that Harper, John D. Rockefeller, Thomas W. Goodspeed, and many others significant in the development of the university were Baptist. The university, in fact, was an outgrowth of pressures brought on Rockefeller by the American Baptist Education Society and was the successor of the defunct University of Chicago (also Baptist), which had failed in 1886 because of insufficient funds.

remained. Harper's crucial distinction, however, was between work that was general, liberal, or preparatory and that which was truly university in nature. Any good junior college or college could provide the former, but only a true university could offer the latter. Harper both regretted and feared the waste which resulted when an institution which was not a university attempted to offer university-level work.

Harper's greatest contribution to the continuing debate over the structure and duration of the baccalaureate program was his support—in action as well as in words—of institutions which offered the first two years of the existing college program: the junior colleges. His basic concern was not whether a secondary institution would offer four or six years of study or whether a small college would offer two or four years beyond high school but whether a true university could eliminate the need to offer the first two years of the traditional baccalaureate program. Harper felt, as had Tappan and Folwell, that the principal distinction was that between preparatory and university studies, and he attempted, through his encouragement of alternate means of offering the first two collegiate years, to reflect this distinction in the offerings of his university. His failure to completely eliminate the first two years from the Chicago campus was due not to a lack of desire but rather to an awareness that the institutions necessary to offer this study were not yet available.

Harper's plans for the division of the collegiate experience and the separation of the first two years from the final two years were an integral part of his plans for the University of Chicago and were announced before the opening of that institution in 1892. At Stanford, however, where President David Starr Jordan also espoused the cause of the junior college, the institution was in operation for sixteen years before Jordan's plans were formally presented to the Board of Trustees in 1907. In the same year, the California legislature passed the first law in the nation to permit "the board of trustees of any city district, union, joint union, or county high school" to "prescribe postgraduate courses of study for the graduates of such high school . . . which courses of study shall approximate the studies prescribed in the first two years of university courses" (cited by Winter, 1964, p. 1).

Jordan was not the first prominent educator in California to promote the separation of junior college work from that of the university. Alexis F. Lange, who had studied at the University of Michigan during the time the experimental university system was in operation, had been trying, since 1892, to foster a reorganization of the University of California which would reflect the distinction between preparatory and university studies. Yet, Lange later admitted that "this propaganda would probably not have gathered momentum very fast without President Jordan's dynamic articles and addresses urging the amputation of freshman and sophomore classes to prevent university atrophy and urging the relegation of these classes to the high school" (cited by Eells, 1931, p. 91). Although no definite evidence has been found of the influence of Jordan or Lange upon the introduction of the legislation by State Senator Anthony Caminetti, Eells (p. 90) concludes that "it may be surmised that the influence of the University of California [Lange] and Stanford University [Jordan] were contributing factors."

Jordan's 1907 report to the trustees of Stanford University was one of the clearest statements of the argument for bisection (pp. 18–22). Beginning with the colleges, "which are English in their origin," and the universities, which "are German in their inspiration and method," Jordan traced the development of American education to the point where "the college has gradually pushed itself upward, relegating its lower years to the secondary schools, and absorbing two of the years which would naturally belong to the university." The result, Jordan concluded, is "a tendency to separate the college into two parts: the junior college of two years, in which the work is still collegiate, and the university college"; yet, "it is better for the university to be as far as possible free from the necessity of junior college instruction."

Jordan, like Harper, did not distinguish between "the college [which might offer this early study], on the one hand, and the graduate courses of the secondary schools on the other." Yet, unlike Harper, Jordan could foresee the day when the institutions necessary to offer this work would be readily available in California. For several years prior to the passage of the 1907 legislation, high schools in California had been offering "postgraduate" work; the legislation simply made this work legal and encouraged other institutions to follow suit. Thus, Jordan recommended to the board "the immediate separation of the junior college from the university or university college" and the requirement of "the work of the junior college as a requisite for admission to the University on and after the year 1913, or as soon as a number of the best equipped high schools of the State are prepared to undertake this work."

The high schools did not respond rapidly enough to allow Stanford to carry through Jordan's recommendations. The first junior college program established in California under the terms of the 1907 legislation began operation at Fresno High School in 1910. In the following year, the first private junior college, Los Angeles Pacific College, was started under the authority of the Free Methodist Church, and three additional public institutions were established, two of them in the Los Angeles area. The University of California opened its southern branch (later the University of California, Los Angeles) in 1919 to offer only lower division courses, but the two post-high school programs in Los Angeles were closed by 1920. As of 1917, ten years after Jordan's first statement to his board, sixteen California high schools were offering postgraduate work with a combined enrollment of over 1,250; yet, over 620 of these students were enrolled in the two Los Angeles institutions which would soon close.

During and after the First World War, the fortunes of the new junior colleges fluctuated greatly. Following the passage, in 1917, of a law to provide state aid for junior college students on a per capita basis and to require a minimum of sixty hours credit for graduation, five additional high schools moved to establish junior college courses; two of these institutions had suspended junior college operations by the end of 1918. By 1919–1920, enrollment had dropped in all California junior colleges to slightly over 1,000 students, and three more college programs had been closed. In the following year, however, five additional high schools began to offer postgraduate work (based on Winter, 1964).

Regardless of these fluctuations, hope continued at Stanford that the lower division could be eliminated. President Ray Lyman Wilbur, in his report of 1920 (pp. 10–11), told the board that Stanford should not continue to waste money "in duplicating work of a grade that is now, or soon will be, handled admirably in forty or fifty institutions within the State," despite the fact that only eighteen such institutions were then in operation. Wilbur supported Jordan's earlier position, although the university had not been able to eliminate its lower division. While reporting that Stanford had just established a lower and upper division to "bring the University in closer harmony with the junior colleges of the State," Wilbur recommended eventually "turning over the teaching of all students up to our present junior year to the junior colleges and like institutions elsewhere."

The state legislature continued to encourage the establishment of junior colleges with the passage, in 1921, of another education law which outlined the mechanism by which junior college districts, similar to high school districts, could be created. This legislation authorized two distinct junior college programs, the high school junior college department (which already existed in eighteen locations) and the newly created district junior college, with different formulas for state support, entrance requirements, and assessed valuation bases. In addition, it gave local governing boards the authority to contract with the state colleges to give junior college courses within a given district.

By 1927, when Wilbur noted (p. 4) that "the quality of instruction in the junior college is at least equal to that given in the university," thirty-one junior colleges were in operation in California; sixteen were departments in high schools, six were being operated by state colleges, and nine were separate district colleges. In view of this "educational tide," Wilbur recommended that Stanford continue to reduce the number of freshmen admitted. "There is no good reason," he wrote, "why endowment funds given for a 'university of high degree' should be used to subsidize elementary instruction given in many places in the state." The board obviously agreed, for the incoming freshman class was again reduced in January 1928.

Despite the apparent growth of the California junior colleges, reaction to Jordan and Wilbur's plans had begun. In May 1927, Wilbur felt it necessary to write all Stanford alumni explaining "certain changes in our educational scheme" which were now required. The Stanford Board of Trustees, in announcing its January decision to further limit freshman enrollment, also reflected alumni protests in its statement that Stanford "has merely decided upon a reduction of admissions to the Lower Division for the academic year 1928–29, and has not reached or announced any decision upon the questions of further reductions or the ultimate elimination of the Lower Division" (cited by Wilbur, 1928, pp. 17–18). Furthermore, five additional junior colleges had closed in 1927 and 1928, and some members of the Stanford administration were raising questions as to the financial loss should the lower division revenues be foregone.

The combination of alumni sentiment and financial questions appears to have settled the issue at Stanford, particularly in view of the rapidly changing economic situation in late 1929. At the same time, the rate of establishment of public junior colleges dwindled rapidly, falling from twenty-three in the decade preceding 1929 to five in the twelve years following that date. At Stanford, as at Chicago, for two decades the president had continuously proposed the abolition of the first two years, but no concrete steps (beyond the limiting of freshman enrollment at Stanford) had been taken. Despite the existence of the most extensive system of public junior colleges in the nation, the advocacy of a bisected college in California appeared to be dead.

John Smart (1967, p. 14) feels that enrollment limits, first adopted in 1916, "precluded the more drastic action" of eliminating the work of the first two years completely at Stanford. Since much of Eells's discussion is aimed at demonstrating support for junior colleges on the part of the Stanford administration (and since Eells was writing before the issue had been permanently decided), it may be that the Smart interpretation is correct. Regardless, enrollment limits did accompany suggestions for the elimination of the lower division between 1916 and 1929; after that time, neither plan was continued.

The failure at Stanford, however, did not prevent continued experimentation with the time structure of the educational system in Chicago, California, and elsewhere. The first junior colleges, in both Illinois and California, were created through the addition of a junior college department to an existing high school, thus forming a six-year program which was, according to Stanley Brown (1908, p. 18), the superintendent of public schools in Joliet, Illinois, "the final step in the complete evolution of the secondary school." If, however, the basic reason for these institutions was to emphasize the "natural division" between the sophomore and junior years of college work, junior colleges did not have to be limited to two years or tied to four-year high schools, as long as they produced a student who had completed two years of college work.

Variations on the major theme of high school, junior college, and college were developed at Chicago through the institution of the Chicago College Plan in 1930, and in other sections of the country through the creation of four-year junior colleges, often developed as part of a six-four-four plan of school organization. The first known four-year junior college was established in Hillsboro, Texas, in 1925 as a reorganization of the existing two-year institution, although the existence of a five-year elementary system meant that the Hillsboro organization resulted not in a six-four-four plan but rather in a five-four-four plan. Thus, five years of elementary school were followed by four years (grades six through nine) of intermediate school, or high school, the entire system being capped by a four-year junior college (grades ten through thirteen). The first community to completely reorganize on a six-four-four basis was Pasadena, California, which voted for the change in 1924 and completed the transformation in 1928 (Eells, 1931, pp. 666–668).

The idea of six-four-four, however, was not new; it had first been advocated in 1894. Moreover, there was no consistency in the pattern of organization for the elementary and secondary years throughout the nation. By 1916, many school districts had shifted from an eight-four plan of organization to a seven-five plan, which allowed for better college preparation and for more comprehensive departmentalization at the high school level. Others were moving toward a six-three-three precollege program, while New York City adopted a six-two-four plan in 1910, giving students the option of vocational school or academic preparation at the start of grade seven. Many of these reforms were based on the assumption that the traditional end of grade eight at age fourteen was both too late to provide for adequate career choice and inappropriate in light of physical and physiological development (based on Bunker, 1916).

On the surface, the arguments for the development of four-year junior colleges were similar to those of Folwell, Tappan, and proponents of junior colleges in general. All seemed to agree that the thirteenth and fourteenth years of education were basically secondary in nature and should not be offered in a collegiate or university setting; moreover, they agreed that the local public educational system might well offer these years to its students. The difference, however, was in the way in which the thirteenth and fourteenth years were to be viewed—and, in consequence, the way in which the curriculum could be structured—as a part of that public educational system. "It is one thing to propose that public school systems take over college functions and do two years of college work," wrote John A. Sexson, superintendent of schools in Pasadena, "and quite another to propose that our public school system be extended to where it may satisfactorily complete the task of secondary education" (cited by Proctor, 1933, p. 19).

By 1929, nine four-year junior colleges were in operation, and the United States Commissioner of Education, William Cooper (1929, p. 346), was advocating a six-four-four plan of school organization "for most American cities and for thickly settled rural areas." Yet, the plan did not spread, in great measure because of the strength of traditional athletics and the fears that this plan might, in the long run, "kill off the historic four-year college by bisecting it disjunctively, that is, by assigning its freshman and sophomore years to secondary schools and its junior and senior years to reorganized universities" (Cowley, 1955, p. 101). These fears were not allayed in the least by statements such as that made by Professor William Campbell (1932, p. 365) of the University of Southern California, a proponent of six-four-four: "It [the four-year junior college] is not a longer and a higher high school; it is not merely the lower portion of the old standard college; it is a new institution, and it is being developed to meet present needs rather than ancient precedents."

The failure of the six-four-four plan to spread in no way diminished some of the cogent arguments in its favor. These arguments were also at the heart of plans for both junior colleges and the possible bisection of the traditional four-year curriculum. President Frank Goodnow (1925, p. 618) of Johns Hopkins, in announcing plans (which were never implemented) to eliminate the first two years from the Johns Hopkins curriculum, found no reason for a university to continue offering "elementary collegiate instruction . . . those courses ordinarily given during the first two years of the American college." These same elementary collegiate courses, when viewed as general education courses, became "the fundamental purpose of the secondary school," according to John Harbeson (1931, p. 8), principal of the Pasadena four-year junior college. Harbeson, like most junior college supporters in these early days, viewed the junior college offerings as an integral part of general education and thus of the public secondary offerings.

Perhaps the clearest equation of junior colleges with the general education offerings of four-year colleges came from President Robert Hutchins of the University of Chicago. In a generally negative article published in 1938—which included such comments as "the junior college is a foreign body in the educational system. . . . It has so far done only a negative job [and] has kept young people from going places and doing things that would have been much worse for them. . . . Public junior colleges are relatively inferior"—Hutchins nonetheless concluded that "as the junior colleges increase in number and develop a good organization and curriculum there will be less and less justification for the maintenance of the freshman and sophomore years in universities." Yet Hutchins stressed the fact that the original junior colleges were not meant to be two-year independent institutions but part of the secondary school on the model of the German gymnasium. The logical outcome, to Hutchins, was a four-year junior college which would eliminate the "anomalous" two-year junior colleges. "Two-year educational units do not exist anywhere else in the world," Hutchins wrote, "and I am inclined to think that we cannot congratulate ourselves on our originality" (pp. 5–9, 11).

Hutchins' preference for a four-year junior college structure was evidenced in deed as well as in word. As early as 1931, the University of Chicago had modified its junior-senior college structure (see the beginning of this chapter), which "had come to have little more significance than that prior to attaining eighteen 'majors' (quarter-courses) of credit the student registered on yellow cards, and after . . . on white cards" (Boucher, 1935, pp. 4, 8). The new system provided that "no specified courses and no stated length of residence are required in the College. The requirements are stated solely in terms of educational attainments, measured by examinations, which may be taken by the Student whenever he and his Dean agree that he is prepared to take them." In accordance with the new plan, the undergraduate offerings of the university were divided into the college (to offer general education) and four "upper divisions" of biological science, humanities, physical science, and social science, each of which offered "specialized education" in a student's chosen field (University of Chicago, 1931, p. 42).

Even before the reorganization, superior students in the university high school had been permitted to take junior college courses offered at the high school for college credit. Two years after the reorganization, the last two years of the university high school were made a part of the administrative structure of the newly created college. Chauncey Boucher (1935, pp. 236–240, 242), dean of the college, gave three reasons for this decision: A separate junior college made little sense since it was often only two more years of high school or a poor duplication of the first two years of college; four years of general college education, as then offered in the United States, was a "wasteful preliminary" to higher education; and the new institution offered a complete general education (grades eleven through fourteen) and so bridged the gap between elementary and higher education. Boucher looked forward to the time when "it may be advisable to frame a continuous and completely integrated program for a consolidated four-year unit."

The new plan at the University of Chicago combined elements of many older plans for educational and structural reform but was probably most similar to that of Tappan, who had proposed that the university recognize that which was of gymnasial, or secondary, nature in its curriculum, even while trying to perfect these particular offerings. In the 1850's Tappan had, however, equated the entire college with the offerings of the gymnasium; by the 1930's, most educators limited it to the first two collegiate years. Hutchins, at Chicago, favored university attempts to perfect these general education offerings if only so the university would affect the high school, rather than the opposite. Other educators throughout the country, especially those who supported the growing junior colleges, whether two or four years, were less concerned with where these offerings were perfected than that they be recognized as separate and different from those which the universities were offering in their third and fourth years.

By 1934, thirty-two years after the establishment of the first public junior college at Joliet, Illinois, 521 junior colleges were in operation in the United States, of which 219, or 42 per cent, were public institutions. Enrollment in junior colleges had just passed 100,000 students and grew, by the end of that depression decade, to over 196,000. Moreover, by the end of the 1930's, over 70 per cent of all junior college students were attending public institutions, which, although established at a decreasing rate during the depression, continued to enroll greater numbers and percentages of students because of their convenience and relatively low tuition rates compared with those of private four-year institutions (Brick, 1964, pp. 24–25).

Equally important, the existence and acceptance of this large and growing number of two-year junior colleges made continuing discussion concerning the appropriate point at which to break the baccalaureate experience superfluous. Educators continued to debate the desirability of dividing the four-year baccalaureate program; for all practical purposes, however, the point at which that division would be made was now set, and in fact the feasibility of operating institutions containing only two years of "collegiate" study had been demonstrated. Whether for the reasons advocated by Folwell, Harper, and Jordan or not, the American college had effectively been divided, at least in those locations where junior colleges flourished.

By the 1930's, too, gradual agreement was being reached on the definitions for the levels of American higher education. The rapid expansion of public secondary education, both in terms of universal availability and of the level of instruction, led to an upgraded and more clearly defined college than that which had existed in the late nineteenth and early twentieth century. Even the work of the freshman and sophomore years, now offered in independent two-year junior colleges often tied to the secondary system, was accepted as being of college level, in part because the concept of a four-year college between secondary and graduate study had finally gained a level of acceptance which protected it against further incursions from the German model of gymnasium and university. Finally, the university itself had taken on many of the organizational aspects envisioned by Folwell—"a federation of schools . . . embracing potentially all subjects of human and practical interest"—and this definition, which emphasized structure as well as level of instruction, diminished the tendency to reject certain courses or subjects as being nonuniversity in nature.

Thus, the stage had been set for the first major successful attempt to completely eliminate the first two years from a four-year institution. Appropriately enough, the attempt occurred in California, where the system of public junior colleges was the most extensive in the nation and where, for over thirty years, officials at the University of California and at Stanford had been advocating such a split. Yet, the change came not at one of these well-established institutions but at an institution in central California which had, throughout its existence, been forced by circumstances "to change and adjust to conditions" which it faced as "a relatively unknown college" (Burns, 1968).

The College of the Pacific, the oldest chartered institution in California, was no newcomer to forced adjustments, although this fact had not diminished the force of the many innovations which the institution had been required to adopt. Originally chartered in July 1851 as California Wesleyan College, the College of the Pacific (which was known as the University of the Pacific between August 1851 and July 1911) became, in 1871, the first California institution to admit women, a decision reached concurrently with the determination to move the institution from Santa Clara to San Jose because of dwindling enrollment. By 1924, the twenty-acre campus in San Jose had become too small to accommodate the expanding enrollment; at the same time, increased competition from other institutions in the area and the construction of a railroad contiguous to the campus led to a decision to seek new quarters elsewhere in the state.

Prior to establishing a new campus, President Tully C. Knoles asked the General Education Board of the Rockefeller Foundation to identify areas of the state in which a private, church-related (Methodist) institution might thrive. The board recommended consideration of the central San Joaquin valley, an area with many high school graduates but no four-year institution of higher education, and the college approached the administrations of several valley cities, including Stockton, Sacramento, and Modesto. The eventual decision to locate the college in Stockton was based, in large measure, upon offers of land by the J. C. Smith Company and of $600,000 by the Stockton Chamber of Commerce; furthermore, both Modesto (1921) and Sacramento (1922) had recently established public junior colleges with which the college would have had to compete. The college was opened for classes, at the third location in its seventy-three year history, in the fall of 1924 (Burns, 1968).

Enrollment at the College of the Pacific grew to a peak of 978 during the 1928–1929 academic year; yet the costs of relocation and the reliance upon tuition for most required funds limited the ability of the institution, even during the years of prosperity, to build an adequate endowment. With the onset of the depression, enrollment (and with it, tuition income) declined, reaching 842 students during the 1931–1932 academic year and 707 the following year. On September 28, 1932, Knoles reported to the Board of Trustees that the college had a "cash deficit of $54,069.58 for the current year . . . [and] it was proposed by the Comptroller that each employee of the College take a two months' cut in salary in addition to the fifteen percent formerly agreed upon" (College of the Pacific, 1925–1939, p. 55).

The College of the Pacific was in a difficult situation, although one not atypical of that of many private institutions during the depths of the depression. On the one hand, enrollment was dropping, in great part because of the financial difficulty involved in college attendance in general and the tuition required at a private institution in particular. The college was not using existing facilities to capacity, although costs involved in taxes and upkeep were not reduced. On the other hand, officials at the institution were loath to make any changes which might affect the academic standing of the college, the one drawing card which remained despite the financial difficulties. Thus, admissions requirements (and tuition) remained high, while enrollment and income were steadily decreasing.[2]

By the opening of the 1933–1934 academic year, the situation was becoming critical, and in October 1933, a special Faculty Coordinating Committee, chaired by Professor J. William Harris, was created to search for possible ways of saving the institution. One solution, suggested by Professor and Debate Coach Dwayne Orton, was that the College of the Pacific establish a separate junior college division without alteration of the traditional four-year curriculum or of the academic standards at the four-year institution. Knoles supported the suggestion and, after having "secured the proper advice from the East" (particularly from Robert Lester of the Carnegie Foundation for the Advancement of Teaching), recommended passage of the junior college proposal at a meeting of the Faculty Coordinating Committee. On March 7, 1934, this committee recommended establishment of a junior college within the College of the Pacific; three weeks later, the Board of Trustees

[2] Knoles (1934a, p. 2) reported that "in spite of our low endowment, our comparatively high tuition rates seem to have been our only salvation. There is, however, always the constant fear that academic standing may be sacrificed to maintain economic life at all, even at a dying rate. We are operating here below capacity in all of our buildings except the Library space, and during the past year we have redoubled our efforts to increase the student body."

approved the plan to establish the College of the Pacific Junior College (Hunt, 1951, p. 148; Knoles, 1934a; College of the Pacific, 1925–1939; Orton, 1968; Bloch, 1962).

Creation of the junior college—the first step toward eventual elimination of the freshman and sophomore years at Pacific— was the culmination of several factors at work both in California and nationally in higher education during the depression. The initial factor was the need to save the college by increasing enrollment and revenues while preserving academic standards. A separate junior college division utilized plant and provided income while having different admissions requirements based on those currently used in public junior colleges throughout California. Moreover, there was "no lowering of our academic standards involved in the experiment, for our recommended (regular) students will not be bothered by having non-recommended students in their classes" (Knoles, 1934a, p. 2).

Yet the creation of an experimental junior college division could be—and was—justified in terms other than those of financial exigencies. For several years, Orton had been studying experimental programs throughout the country, with a view toward reform of the general education offerings at Pacific. As stated in the first catalogue of the junior college, "The Junior College of the College of the Pacific was organized in response to a long felt need for a general liberal educational unit to provide a broad intellectual training and an appreciative view of modern life under the auspices and influence of a Christian College." Moreover, recognizing current educational thinking—at least in Chicago, California, and Texas— the catalogue stated that "the Junior College is in line with the trend in American liberal education which recognized the first two years of the arts college as the concluding period of the student's general education" (College of the Pacific, 1934, p. 2).

The new College of the Pacific Junior College opened, with Orton as director, in the fall of 1934 with sixty-five students who, because of the lower admissions requirements, "otherwise would not be at College of the Pacific" (Knoles, 1934b, p. 2). Of equal importance, the junior college students paid a flat fee of seven dollars per semester unit, and "had it not been for our Junior College offerings . . . our freshman class would have been the smallest in our history on the Stockton campus" (Knoles, 1935, p. 1). Nonetheless, this new enrollment was not as great as had been hoped for or anticipated, and Knoles suggested that the Faculty Coordinating Committee consider other steps to increase enrollment.

A first step, taken in the early spring of 1935, was an attempt to secure legislation authorizing county superintendents of schools of the state to pay tuition for students attending the College of the Pacific Junior College. Although this bill would have enabled the college to compete financially with the public junior colleges, it "was not brought on the floor [of the State legislature] for consideration," Knoles (1935, p. 2) reported to his board, "through fear of unconstitutionality." The next step was to consider establishment of a public junior college using the underutilized facilities and faculty at Pacific. On June 10, 1935, Knoles reported that "he had been informed that it would be entirely legal for the Stockton High School unit under its Board of Education to organize itself into a High School-Junior College District . . . [and] to rent such buildings or rooms of the College of the Pacific as would be designated for the use of the Junior College" (College of the Pacific, 1925–1939, pp. 123, 127).

Exactly when Knoles first considered establishment of a public junior college in a cooperative arrangement with the College of the Pacific is unclear. In his report of October 1935 (p. 2) (after the new public institution had opened), he explained that "for a number of years various education leaders in the state have commented upon the possibility of the organization of public junior college classes on the part of the Stockton School Board in connection with the College of the Pacific." Orton (1968) has stated that Knoles discussed with him the possibility of a "coordinate arrangement of public and private institutions" as early as the spring of 1934 during early consideration of the College of the Pacific Junior College. Perhaps Knoles's initial idea in 1934 was to admit students financed by the state to the new College of the Pacific Junior College; indeed, his October report indicates that such an arrangement was favored by local educational leaders as well as by himself. Nonetheless, with the decision that this procedure would be declared unconstitutional and with continued "public sentiment to inaugurate Junior College classes, either in the Stockton High School, or through the setting up of a Public Junior College," Knoles decided that the College of the Pacific should support efforts for a public institution and eliminate its own freshman and sophomore offerings.

In July 1935 Knoles formally presented to the Stockton Board of Education his offer to provide space on the College of the Pacific campus for local students being educated at that time at Modesto, Sacramento, and San Mateo junior colleges, an arrangement which was costing Stockton residents over $30,000 each year in tuition paid to other junior college districts. The Stockton school board passed a resolution asking the state to approve the prescribing of junior college courses in the Stockton High School District (Stockton Board of Education, 1931–1937). Although no mention was made of an agreement with the College of the Pacific, informal discussions among representatives of the college and the state had already determined that rental of college buildings by a public institution would be entirely legal. Moreover, both the Stockton school board and the College of the Pacific assumed that a rental agreement would benefit both institutions (Orton, 1968).

With informal information from Sacramento that its petition would be approved, the Stockton school board resolved on August 23, 1935, to open its new junior college for first year students during that fall semester. On October 3, the formal rental agreement with the College of the Pacific was approved by the school board, and on October 15, final state approval was received. A local citizen, Ansel S. Williams, was appointed director of the new public Stockton Junior College (Orton was still director of the College of the Pacific Junior College), and the institution opened two weeks later with 301 students (Stockton Board of Education, 1931–1937).

The faculty and staff of the College of the Pacific were also extremely busy during the summer of 1935 preparing for the eventual transfer of their lower division functions to the public institution, although few believed that the public institution could be approved and opened before the fall of 1936. As an intermediate step toward this transfer, the Faculty Coordinating Committee recom-

mended on October 16, 1935—one day after state approval for the
public junior college had been received—creation of a "general
college" within the College of the Pacific (Hunt, 1951, p. 149).
This "reorganized lower division of the College of the Pacific . . .
[was] organized to administer the work of the freshman and sophomore years" and incorporated the old (one-year) College of the
Pacific Junior College, as well as the "regular" freshman and sophomore classes. The general college was scheduled to begin its operations in the fall of 1936; its courses were to stress "those common
elements of human culture which have intrinsic value for the human race" and were, in fact, very similar to the general survey
courses then being offered by the College of the Pacific Junior College (College of the Pacific, 1935, pp. 3, 5, 6).

Thus, as of October 1935, the public junior college—Stockton Junior College—was in operation for freshmen only, with sophomores to be admitted in the fall of 1936, and the College of the
Pacific Junior College was offering classes for both freshmen and
sophomores. The College of the Pacific itself had just admitted
another freshman class—the opening of Stockton Junior College
having come too late to affect this decision—and was providing
education to four classes in its regular program. Finally, a decision
was reached to combine the College of the Pacific Junior College
with the first two years of the regular program, creating a general
college, which itself would be phased out at its inception in September 1936 by not admitting any new freshmen.

The apparent confusion and duplication of planning efforts
were the result of the rapidity with which events had moved during
the summer and fall of 1935. Although the College of the Pacific
had been committed since March 1935 to support a public institution—and to the concomitant need to eliminate its own offerings at
the freshman and sophomore levels—there had been no indication
that the public junior college could or would be begun as quickly
as it was. In any case, Knoles was not adverse to a reorganization
of his own institution which would provide for a distinct separation
between the sophomore and junior years, regardless of the outcome
of the public junior college experiment. In fact, with the public
college in its second year of operation, he wrote (1936, p. 5) that

"we can now do what many educators have long contended should be done, concentrate upon the work of the Upper Division and graduate year, frankly recognizing in fact what is recognized in law in California that the Lower Division is a part of secondary education."

Of equal importance, Knoles saw creation of a public institution in a contractual arrangement with the College of the Pacific as a step necessary to save the college, as well as one which would be advantageous to the community of Stockton. Public pressure for community college offerings not tied to the strict entrance requirements at College of the Pacific had been one reason for the initial establishment of the College of the Pacific Junior College, although this arrangement did not provide adequate opportunities for local citizens since the tuition was set at the normal level. Moreover, there had been hints of legislative pressure on San Joaquin County to establish a junior college since "Stockton by virtue of its size and assessed valuation is clearly entitled to have junior college classes under any of the state possibilities, Joint Union, County, Junior College District or Junior College classes provided by a High School Board" (Knoles, 1936, p. 3). Yet establishment of a public college in competition with College of the Pacific, especially during the depths of the depression, would have been disastrous.

The final decision to eliminate the lower division and to view Stockton Junior College as the equivalent of the freshman and sophomore years was also a financial windfall for the College of the Pacific. Not only did it no longer need to support the operations of a full four-year institution under its own budget, but it received additional income from the rental of presently underutilized facilities to the public junior college. Combined with Knoles's beliefs about the proper administrative and educational organization of higher education and the reasons for establishment of a new public junior college, these financial reasons created arguments for cooperative arrangements which could not be ignored.

The result was a four-year academic program—offered on a single campus to a single student body—administered and supported by two independent institutions of higher education, one public and one private. The potential for successful cooperation between the two institutions was greatly increased when, on May 27, 1936, Orton, director of the College of the Pacific Junior College, was named to replace Williams as dean of Stockton Junior College (Stockton Board of Education, 1931–1937). Orton continued the active recruiting efforts begun by Williams, and by September 1936 enrollment at the new junior college had reached 860, an increase of 559 from its first year of operation.

The merging of the offerings of the two institutions into a single academic program had begun with the decision, made early in the development of the public college, to employ many College of the Pacific faculty in the junior college, thus providing quality teachers for the new college and increased financial compensation for the underpaid faculty, all of whom were receiving less than one-half their 1929 base pay from the College of the Pacific. The fact that the two colleges shared buildings and facilities under the rental agreement of October 1935 added to the impression that one academic institution existed. The final step in this process was taken on December 10, 1936, when the students of both institutions voted to create a single student body and a unified student organization, the Pacific Students Association (*Pacific Weekly,* 1936, p. 1). By the end of the 1936–1937 academic year, the managers of both the *Pacific Weekly,* the student newspaper, and the *Pacific Year Book* were junior college students (Orton, n.d.).

The institutions remained distinct, however, in two important aspects. Each was a separate legal and corporate entity, responsible to its own board (the Stockton Board of Education and the Board of Trustees of the College of the Pacific) and with its own independent financing, although a significant part of the Pacific income was derived from rental payments received from Stockton Junior College. Moreover, although "students are admitted to the Junior College rather freely, much more freely than was the case in the lower division of the College . . . only those with a 'C' average in courses leading to the Junior standing are admitted to the Senior College" (Knoles, 1937, p. 2). Yet even this academic distinction was occasionally blurred, as when Knoles, in reporting to his board on the enrollment at the junior college, stated that "our enrollment" was greater than had been expected.

On April 1, 1937, Knoles (p. 3) reported, "My enthusiasm for our enterprise grows with experience. The College is realizing much more fully upon its facilities, all competition for students in the lower division is removed, and an adequate base for the Senior College is fairly assured. Strife could arise, but if frank understanding is practiced I can see nothing but continued good." In fact, the College of the Pacific continued to operate as an upper division institution for sixteen years, until circumstances, including a lack of "frank understanding" between Stockton Junior College and the College of the Pacific, led to a decision to reinstitute the freshman and sophomore years. For at least a decade, the College of the Pacific operated successfully as the first upper division institution in the nation, while the local junior college provided the work of the first two collegiate years, work which Folwell, Harper, Jordan, and Knoles believed should not be the province of an institution of true university stature.

Three

The War Years

Although the depression caused severe hardships in many American institutions of higher education, it provided at least one institution, the New School for Social Research, with a unique opportunity for expansion and service. At the beginning of the 1930's, the New School was a relatively disorganized forum for individual lectures and other forms of adult education; by the end of the decade, it offered an unusual graduate degree program and soon opened an upper division college, itself unique in its philosophy, faculty, students, and course offerings. Since its inception, the New School had been distinctive, and each of these developments stemmed logically from the basic assumptions and goals upon which the school had been created in the fall of 1918 and the spring of 1919.

The original adult education programs at the New School

were developed to meet a special situation, according to Alvin Johnson (1968), cofounder and long-time director of the New School. These programs, a direct outgrowth of the lyceums and Chautauqua which had flourished at the turn of the last century, were a result of the inability of many established institutions of higher education during the First World War to offer a forum for full and open discussion of controversial issues. Thus, a controversy over academic freedom at Columbia led to the resignation of Charles Beard and James Harvey Robinson, two of the original members of the New School faculty; they and other distinguished educators, including John Dewey, Roscoe Pound, Thorstein Weblen, and Herbert Crowly, felt the "need of a new institution which should be honestly free." The New School for Social Research, which opened on February 9, 1919, was to be such an institution (Johnson, 1952, p. 273).

Above all, the New School was to be an institution for adults, where students desiring learning for the sake of learning could attend lectures and classes, unhampered by a structure of credits or degree requirements. It was to be, according to Robinson's ideals, a haven for scholars who could speak to the educated public; according to Beard, it was to be a center for research, unhindered by the necessity to provide a given number of class hours each week or by the public-relations-oriented demands of an overbearing Board of Trustees. Initially, the New School was all of these things; sadly, disagreements among Crowly, Beard, and Robinson as to the emphasis to be placed upon research and teaching and the role of the Board of Trustees eventually led to the resignation, in 1923, of all three men. At that point, Johnson became the first full-time director in an effort to hold the school together despite the resignation of its two best known lecturers (Johnson, 1952, pp. 273, 281).

The New School did manage to survive, primarily because of the efforts of Johnson and the lectures of Weblen, and reached its golden age in the late 1920's. In 1930, it moved into its first permanent building but "the auspices were not the best" and "the economic crisis was proceeding remorselessly" (Johnson, 1952, p. 228). Student enrollments began to fall off drastically, and three years later, the institution was in serious financial difficulty. Yet, American was not the only nation in the grips of a depression, and events in Europe soon provided an unequaled opportunity for a unique experiment in education, the New School University in Exile.

Johnson first conceived the University in Exile in the early 1930's to provide refuge for European scholars who were finding the intellectual and academic climate in their countries increasingly oppressive. With Hitler's ascent to power in Germany in 1933, Johnson and Emil Lederer, an Austrian economist, developed the idea of bringing large numbers of German scholars to the United States. Rather than providing simply an academic immigration service, however, they dreamed of providing a centralized location in which the scholars could re-create the ideals of a European university. Concurrently, Johnson dreamed of creating a true graduate faculty as a capstone to the educational offerings of the New School. Primarily through the generosity of Hiram Halle, a New York businessman who provided $120,000 to support the venture, the faculty of the University in Exile was assembled in New York in the summer of 1933. Among its members were Hans Speier, Albert Salomon, Max Ascoli, and Karl Mannheim; the next year, a new group of scholars, including Hans Simons (future president of the New School), arrived (Johnson, 1952, pp. 337–346).

Thus, an institution that had begun as a group of prominent American scholars giving lectures to an adult public had overnight added a graduate faculty composed of some of the finest European scholars. Concurrently, the old avoidance of credits and degrees was threatened; a graduate faculty required the ability to offer graduate degrees if it was to secure the students with which it could prosper. The New School petitioned the State Education Department in Albany for a charter and, on June 22, 1934, received a provisional charter under which the Master and Doctor of Social Science were awarded by the University of the State of New York upon recommendation by the graduate faculty (the University in Exile) of the New School for Social Research (New School, 1934–1945).

From the outset, however, the graduate faculty created additional problems for the New School. Johnson (1952, p. 348) be-

lieved "that while the faculty as a unit would become assimilated
to American conditions, the group organization would protect the
individual member against the conventional mutilating process of
individual assimilation." Johnson's desire to preserve the individu-
ality of the graduate faculty, as a group, led, in 1936, to the creation of a separate Board of Trustees for the graduate faculty. Thus
"from the outset, the Graduate Faculty was an integral part of the
New School but an independent entity within the School" (Swift,
1952, p. II-40). As seen by Simons (1968), the University in Exile
was a homogeneous and somewhat introspective group of exiles operating within, but not as an integral part of, the New School.

The feelings that the New School was becoming somewhat
disjointed—a mere collection of free-floating organizations under a
single director—played an important role in the ultimate creation
of the New School Senior College in 1944; in the late 1930's, however, they were not verbalized concerns. Moreover, more work on
behalf of European scholars was required. Hitler's invasion of Czech-
oslovakia and the subsequent fall of France and Belgium led Johnson once again into the area of immigration, this time to create the
École Libre des Hautes Études. Through the generosity of the Rockefeller Foundation and with the cooperation of General Charles de
Gaulle, "who accepted the institution as the one Free French university then in existence," the École Libre provided refuge for such
Gallic scholars as Gustav Cohen, Jacques Maritain, and Boris Mir-
kine-Guetzevitch (Johnson, 1952, pp. 367–372).

The creation of yet another independent organization within
the New School and the possibility of combining several of the institutes into a World Institute led, in late 1942 and early 1943, to
"many months of deliberation on the reorganization of the New
School." Johnson reported to his board, on April 14, 1943, that
"the New School as such had no organization." Yet "on the inside
of the School one element was clearly defined. The Graduate Faculty was autonomous under its Dean, the Dean was responsible to
the Director, and the Director to the Board." Johnson's recommendations, approved by the board, were that the divisions of the
school, with the exception of the Institute of World Affairs and the
École Libre, should be organized "for administrative convenience"

into a School of Politics and a School of Philosophy and Liberal
Arts; the graduate faculty was divided along the same lines, although it retained its own dean and Board of Trustees (until 1946)
(New School, 1934–1945). Simons was named dean of the School
of Politics, while the School of Philosophy and Liberal Arts was
under the direction of Clara Mayer, one of the original students
and then associate director.

One basic purpose of the reorganization was to provide a
structure in which adults—still the primary focus—could receive
a truly liberal education. Although most students still took only
those courses which interested them in whatever order they desired,
there was, "for those who desire it," an opportunity for guided
study. "On the average, 30 semester courses, added to previous education and experience, may be considered as fulfilling the requirements of a 'liberal education.' " Upon completion of the liberal
education work, a student "may receive a certificate" (New School,
1943, p. 15); this freedom of choice and the general lack of organization in providing course choices were, according to Johnson, "one
of the most interesting experiments, the attempt to give a really liberal education on the adult level" (New School, 1934–1945).

Yet the new organization had not resolved the problem of
integrating the graduate faculty into the institution; Simons (1968),
in particular, felt that the graduate faculty required an underpinning to bring it into contact with the institution as a whole and
with general students in particular. Johnson (1968), noting a
"pretty scanty" enrollment in the graduate degree programs, was
in favor of some means "to equip students who had been drop
outs . . . to . . . reach the level where they could enter the graduate programs." The result, developed by Simons from an idea by
Lederer, the dean of the faculty, was the creation of the New School
Senior College.

The specific event which appears to have coalesced these divergent dissatisfactions was the introduction in Congress of the G.I.
bill in early 1944. Under this legislation, signed into law on June
22, 1944, the federal government provided financial support for
veterans who wished to further their education; of equal importance to those at the New School, the returning veterans repre-

sented a newly opening reservoir of mature and experienced students with whom the members of the graduate faculty could be expected to communicate. As stated by Simons in March 1944, "The New School wants to be of service in the federal program for the education of returning soldiers and . . . wish[es] to fulfill any requirements [for the State Department of Education] necessary to qualify us for participation in the program" (cited by New School, 1934–1945).

According to Simons' report to the Board of Trustees, the initial reaction of New York State Commissioners George Stoddard and J. Hillis Miller was that the New School itself should not offer a degree program but should establish a cooperative arrangement with Columbia University or the City College of New York to have one of those institutions validate course work offered at the New School and to offer the necessary degree credit. Stoddard believed that the New School, without laboratory facilities and with essentially an adult student body, could not develop a strong four-year degree program. Simons, accepting these reasons as being basically correct, countered with the proposal that the New School, admitting its shortcomings in the laboratory areas and its desire for older students, open a senior college which would require two years of previous college work for admission. The state immediately endorsed this plan, especially since Stoddard was planning for twenty junior colleges of applied arts and science throughout the state and saw a senior college as providing a possible capstone to this new educational system (New School, 1934–1945).

Thus, agreement was reached, although what the state saw as a capstone for future junior college students the New School saw as an opportunity "to underpin the structure of the Graduate Faculty by connecting it with a small number among the whole student body who can be prepared for graduate work" (New School, 1934–1945). The ability to begin this baccalaureate program at the junior year would mean not only a more mature student body—in keeping with the traditions of the New School—but also that the program, by avoiding laboratory work usually required in the first two years, could reduce its costs, which then could be met mainly out of credit fees provided for the veterans by the government.

Finally, the decision of the state to approve the program "on the basis of the wartime emergency" meant less rigorous demands for the structure of the program and allowed the New School to retain its basic schedule of course offerings and to integrate the baccalaureate students into those courses already available.

Of central importance to the New School was the ability, under the arrangements worked out with the state, to offer a program which would continue to serve what was primarily an adult population (Simons, 1968). Even so, there was still some opposition to the introduction of any undergraduate degree program, especially among those from the original group who had migrated to the New School with Robinson and Beard in revolt against the academic twenty years earlier. "As far as can be seen," Simons assured his hesitant colleagues, "the 'senior college' part of our program, though it will demand full attention, will always be a sideline rather than the center of our activities" (cited by New School, 1934–1945).

On May 19, 1944, the Board of Regents of the State of New York granted an amendment to the New School charter and empowered the New School to grant the Bachelor of Arts degree. The request of the New School for this amendment justified the change as an experimental program to meet postwar needs, although the amendment was not limited to the postwar period, nor did it specify that the baccalaureate program would always be limited to two years in length. As if to emphasize the sideline nature of the baccalaureate program, the new catalogue, in which the first announcement of the new program was made, contained a three-sentence announcement. Following the statement that the charter had been amended, the announcement concluded: "A special folder giving detailed information is available on request. Adults who have successfully completed two years of college education or its equivalent can be admitted for study toward this degree" (New School, 1944, p. 18).

The new senior college was opened for students in the fall of 1944. Twelve half-time faculty members—six in the social sciences and six in the humanities—were engaged with the cooperation of the New York City colleges and universities where they were teaching; many of these professors, however, were already teaching at the New School, and the creation of the senior college program did not significantly alter the course offerings of the New School. Many of the initial students—no numbers are available for the first two years of operation, an additional indication of the informality with which the program was conducted—were full time, although a majority of students soon chose to take only one or two courses each semester as employment opportunities increased after the war. In the fall of 1946 119 baccalaureate students were registered for at least one course; by the fall of 1947, approximately fifteen students had completed a satisfactory program of study and had received the baccalaureate degree.

One additional reason for the decision to operate the college in this manner—although never stated by any of the principals—might well have been the background of those involved in the creation of the New School Senior College. Lederer, Simons, and the vast majority of the graduate faculty had come to the United States with the University in Exile; their entire background and training had been in the great German universities, where competent, mature students, having completed a rigorous preparation in the gymnasia, came for an independent intellectual experience known as higher education. Thus, it was perfectly normal to develop a program in which the student was expected to have completed his general education before coming to the college, the major function of which was to provide a selection of courses and whatever guidance the student might desire.

Furthermore, Johnson's thinking was centered—as it had been for twenty-five years—on the graduate and the adult student; "the adolescents could come along after their needs had been taken care of." For Johnson (1968), "the adult mind is essentially different from the juvenile mind; the former is all for acquisition while the latter is all for preparation." Given the history of the New School, the background of its faculty, and the predisposition of its president, it is not at all surprising that an upper division institution, modeled (consciously or not) on the German university, should have developed. The only major question was the timing; the introduction of the G.I. bill and the felt need on the part of Johnson and Simons for internal organizational reforms at the New School provided the answer.

One may also question the effect other educational developments in the United States might have had upon the decisions taken at the New School. Simons and Johnson were totally unaware of the experiment started eight years earlier at the College of the Pacific; Johnson (1968) was "aware and uninterested" in the early twentieth century theoretical developments concerning the appropriate time and the division of courses for a collegiate education. According to Simons (1968), the new senior college was not consciously modeled on any other institution, primarily because the preferred clientele was not the regular high school graduate, age eighteen to twenty, but the older and more mature adult who returned in order to continue his education—the student who had been the central concern of the New School since its inception.

Thus, the New School continued its tradition of providing special educational services to specific, identifiable groups within the general population, primarily adults and those interested in education for its own sake. The decision to establish an upper division program to serve adults and returning veterans was not a result, as it was at other universities during the 1950's and 1960's, of pressures brought upon the institution from new constituencies, particularly the increasing numbers of junior college graduates. Although national junior college enrollment had grown to over half a million by the end of the Second World War, New York State had just begun its development of a system of junior colleges which would enroll 45,000 full-time students by 1964. Even in the 1960's, when the New School modified its senior college to create a new upper division institution, the primary concern was still with groups of students other than the junior college graduates.

Nationwide, however, the junior college movement was rapidly gaining ground. The end of the war and the return of veterans played a part in the increase of both institutions and enrollment; more important, however, was the growing feeling, recognized and fostered by the 1947 report of the President's Commission on Higher Education, that "American colleges . . . can no longer consider themselves merely the instrument for producing an intellectual elite;

they must become the means by which every citizen, youth, and adult is enabled and encouraged to carry his education, formal and informal, as far as his native capacities permit." Furthermore, rapidly expanding industries and changing technologies, themselves a product of the war, created new needs for middle-level technicians which the junior colleges moved to fill. In so doing, the junior colleges entered the second major phase of their development. No longer were they to be simply the equivalent of the first two collegiate years; they now provided a new kind of vocational and technological education to supply manpower for a growing range of technological needs.

The changing role of junior colleges had important ramifications in the establishment of upper division institutions. Early junior colleges, particularly those advocated and supported by William R. Harper and David S. Jordan, had been established to offer the first two years of collegiate (or the last two years of preparatory) education. Although Harper had also envisioned a role for the four-year liberal arts college, he had hoped that a growing system of junior colleges would allow the universities to rid themselves of these years and to concentrate on their own university-level work. Most universities, however, had been loath to give up their freshman and sophomore years, which were financially the most rewarding, and the junior colleges had developed as an additional unit, existing alongside the colleges and universities, whose first two years they duplicated.

Until the Second World War, only California had developed an extensive system of public junior colleges; states such as New York, Florida, Texas, and Michigan, which developed comprehensive systems of junior colleges by the late 1950's, were just beginning, during and after the war, to establish them. Following the war, the expansion of vocational and technical offerings in the junior colleges created a new justification for the existence of these institutions; concurrently, the emphasis on community colleges (with appropriate community service) rather than on junior colleges increased the role which the two-year colleges played. Universities still could (and would) decide to eliminate their own basic offerings based on the availability of junior college education, but they no longer had to justify bisection of a four-year baccalaureate program first. Junior colleges continued to offer the first two years for those students interested in transfer to baccalaureate-granting institutions, but their role (and with it their accepance by the general public) had been greatly expanded by the addition of large-scale technical, non-transfer-oriented programs.

With this change, consideration of establishing upper division institutions was based on a different set of questions from those which concerned Tully C. Knoles at Pacific and Simons at the New School. Bisection and its relationship to the roles of secondary and university education were no longer primary issues; university planners could turn to other considerations, such as the technological, sociological, and demographic needs of their own area. Increasingly, upper division colleges became the concern of public, rather than private, institutions, especially since public universities were often committed to providing baccalaureate education for those students initially educated in public junior colleges. Furthermore, public institutions were more susceptible to pressures from developing industries or from constituencies demanding baccalaureate education than were the private institutions which had led the way in the development of upper division colleges.

Even before the war had ended, however, a private institution, the University of Chicago, announced a new plan of organization which once again put it at the center of a violent educational controversy. In 1931, the university had modified its junior-senior college structure by creating a lower division college and four specialized upper divisions; in 1933, the last two years of the university high school were made a part of the administrative structure of the newly created college (see Chapter Two). Then, in January 1942 —partially because of educational theories and partially to provide an accelerated baccalaureate program to meet wartime needs— President Robert M. Hutchins proposed that the University of Chicago and all other institutions of higher education offer the baccalaureate degree at the end of the traditional sophomore year of college.

"Few actions of the University have caused more discussion," Hutchins wrote in 1949, "than the relocation of the Bachelor's degree" (p. 7). This remark was certainly an understatement. Within a few months, the decision had been condemned by the Association of American Colleges, the National Association of State Universities, the National Conference of Church-Related Colleges, the Association of Colleges and Universities of the Pacific Southwest, the North Central Association of Colleges and Secondary Schools, and the American Association of University Women (Tolley, 1942). Yet Hutchins continued in his 1949 statement, "few [actions] have been more satisfactory in their educational results."

Hutchins' basic reasoning was simple and was logically derived from the steps taken previously in the reorganization of the University of Chicago. Hutchins was concerned, as was Johnson at the New School, with providing a liberal education; Hutchins' reasoning, however, was more closely related to that of Jordan at Stanford or Knoles at the College of the Pacific. Following the reorganization of 1931 and 1933, Hutchins concluded, probably correctly, that the liberal education function of most colleges was concluded by the end of the sophomore year, at which point the student began his specialization, or university, work. "An institution which wishes to disentangle the university and the college must fix the point at which the college ends and the university begins," Hutchins wrote, "in conformity to some notion of the aim of collegiate as distinguished from university work" (1942, p. 567).

Although some educators were still concerned with distinguishing collegiate from university work and agreed with Hutchins' initial statement, few agreed with the conclusions which Hutchins proceeded to draw. "The B.A. degree," Hutchins wrote in a statement reminiscent of those of Francis Wayland nearly a century earlier, "had come to stand merely for four years' attendance after high school at an educational institution" instead of the completion of a student's liberal education. The master's degree, which formerly "represented little but a year's attendance at a graduate school" (1949, pp. 7, 8), would be awarded three years after completion of the baccalaureate to represent competency in a specialization. Under present conditions, according to Hutchins, both the bachelor's and the master's degrees were "conferred at the wrong point for the wrong reasons" (1942, p. 571).

Hutchins' critics, although in agreement that the "change is *undesirable, unnecessary,* and *unfortunate*" (Eells, 1942a, p. 355), disagreed among themselves as to why the change was so terrible. W. E. Peik, dean of the College of Education at the University of Minnesota, was willing to concede that many high school and junior college offerings were providing "the same opportunity to get introductory courses in the principal fields of human activity and culture" but felt that the baccalaureate itself did "signify much more than one or two years of cultural education as represented by the junior college." The solution, according to Peik, was reform at the secondary and junior college level; although agreeing with some of Hutchins' goals, Peik nonetheless felt that the "step was ill-advised and will lead to confusion" rather than to a solution of any of the basic problems (1942, pp. 363, 370). Walter Crosby Eells, executive secretary of the American Association of Junior Colleges, agreed (1942b) that the baccalaureate signified more than simply two years of college; one of his prime concerns, however, was the meaning of the more than three million baccalaureates held in the United States if Hutchins' ideas were to spread.

C. H. Faust (1942), dean of the college at the University of Chicago, countered the arguments that the plan would rob the baccalaureate of its significance with the statement that much of the acceleration being encouraged because of the wartime demand for manpower had already led to a loss of meaning for the baccalaureate degree. The University of Chicago would reestablish a meaning for the degree—the completion of a liberal education—and might even eliminate the need for extensive acceleration once an appropriate stopping point short of the full four years of college was provided for those who did not want or need specialization.

The question of appropriate recognition of the end of a liberal education, however, was another sore point, especially with Eells and other proponents of junior colleges. Eells (1942b) agreed that it was necessary to "dignify this important point of educational achievement with a significant college degree . . . [but] not *the bachelor's degree*." A well-established degree already existed, Eells reminded Hutchins, to signify the end of the work of the lower division; the University of Chicago, in fact, had been the first institution (1900) to award an associate degree for this purpose. Even admitting that a liberal education should, in fact, be offered in a program combining the eleventh through the fourteenth years, as was to be done at Chicago, Eells felt that the associate degree was still appropriate, as it was at the four-year junior college in Pasadena.

Hutchins had not recommended simply that four-year institutions recognize the end of liberal education through the use of what came to be known as "Hutchins' two-year baccalaureate" but had added that all junior colleges should offer the baccalaureate degree for their two years of liberal education. Very few junior colleges supported the opportunity to upgrade their degree offerings. According to Eells, only 8 per cent of all junior colleges in the country viewed the possibility favorably (1942a, p. 357), despite Hutchins' statement that any institution "that wants to develop liberal education must mark its completion by that [the baccalaureate] degree" (1942, p. 570).[1]

The issue was not resolved for over a decade, as the University of Chicago and the American educational system went separate ways, each convinced of the correctness of its position. Yet the issue was significant if for no other reason than that it provided one of the few opportunities for national discussion of problems relating to the organization and timing of the baccalaureate degree. For the first time in many years, a prominent American educator had questioned the basic assumptions on which the traditional four-year baccalaureate was based and had arrived at a significantly different plan of organization for an American institution, a plan which harked back to the original contentions of Henry Tappan and Wayland that a university was significantly different from a secondary or collegiate institution.

Although Hutchins did not mention the German model on

[1] The appellation "Hutchins' two-year baccalaureate" reflected a complete misunderstanding of Hutchins' intent. He did not want to create a two-year baccalaureate degree but to offer the baccalaureate after completion of the first two years of college work. Ideally, other institutions would model their programs on that at Chicago, where these first two collegiate years were closely tied to the last two years of high school, creating a four-year unit reminiscent of that in the Pasadena six-four-four program.

which his proposals might have been based, at least one educator, Richard Gummere, director of admissions at Harvard, saw this model, if only to dispute it. "Our graduate schools are of course modelled on the German idea, for many reasons," Gummere wrote, "but the parallel holds only in the graduate years *per se* and not in the undergraduate course" (1942, p. 344). In reality, however, the last two years of the American undergraduate course were modeled, at least in terms of methodology, on the German universities of the nineteenth century; reliance on the German model had been a primary cause of earlier disagreement as to the ultimate structure that the American college should adopt. Moreover, at least one system of education in the United States was modeled, at all levels, on the German system: that of the Evangelical Lutheran Synod of Missouri, Ohio, and Other States, now known as the Lutheran Church—Missouri Synod.

This system, begun in 1839 with the establishment of a theological seminary and supporting college in Perry County, Missouri, "took the standard program of studies of the theological faculty of a German university as the pattern for the seminary and that of the German classical gymnasium as the pattern for the pre-professional college." In 1860, the college, then known as the Concordia Gymnasium or Collegium, moved to Fort Wayne, Indiana, where it was still in operation in 1944 with a six-year preprofessional curriculum leading to admission to the seminary, then located in St. Louis, Missouri.[2]

Throughout the remainder of the nineteenth century and the first third of the twentieth, no attempt was made to change the basic classical curricular or organizational pattern within the synodical system of education, and "there appears to have been no conscious attempt, even though the designation 'college' was used, to accommodate the pre-professional school to the pattern of the contemporary American college." In the wake of the many German-Lutheran immigrants who came to the United States before the First World War, several new preparatory schools were established; each of these institutions was organized, as was Concordia College,

[2] Factual material concerning Concordia Senior College is drawn from Concordia Senior College, 1961, pp. 7–11.

as a six-year program leading to seminary study. Thus, it is not surprising that "the faculties looked to the classical gymnasium of Germany rather than to the American liberal arts college as a source of inspiration."

A synodical commission, reporting in 1920 on possible changes needed in the educational system following the First World War, failed to follow the lead of other Lutheran bodies in accommodating their institutions of higher education to the standard American college patterns. The commission did recommend, however, that the word *gymnasium* be dropped from all institutional names and replaced with the designations of high school (for the first four years) and junior college (for the last two years). Yet "very little happened to the existing pattern; it was only the name of the schools that was changed."

Not until 1935, after two years of study, was the first major change in the century-old system of synodical education made with the extension of the seminary course from three to four years and the decision to award the baccalaureate degree after the second seminary year (or the fourth year of higher education). At the same time, changes were made in the curricula of the junior colleges; less time was allotted to classical languages, and survey courses, patterned after those instituted at the University of Chicago in the early 1930's, were introduced in several nonreligious subjects.

The attempt by the church to solve its problems of ministerial education—the primary purpose of its entire educational system—by extending the course of study at the seminary and by including some liberal arts work in the first two years did not prove satisfactory. By 1940, demands for a reconsideration of the basic structure of the educational system—partially to bring it into line with the American system, thus facilitating transfer among institutions and entrance to other graduate schools, partially to provide a broader education for the ministry, and partially as a result of the new growth and role of American junior colleges—had become more insistent from within the church (Evangelical Lutheran Synod of Missouri, Ohio, and Other States, 1947, pp. 152–154).

The entry of the United States into the Second World War made the need for reform even more urgent as the synod discovered that a four-year college course with a recognized baccalaureate degree was required for appointments to chaplaincies in the Armed Forces. Furthermore, whereas only sixteen theological schools had required the baccalaureate for admission in 1924, by 1940 all accredited theological schools—the synod seminary was not accredited —required it. Thus, "fully aware of the plannings and discussion coming out of the University of Chicago under President Hutchins' leadership in the early forties," members of the Board for Higher Education of the synod once again began to consider a restructuring of the system of education. "We were encouraged, of course," Martin J. Neeb (1968b), executive secretary of the board from 1945 to 1955, has stated, "by the fact that a reputable university [the University of Chicago] was willing to examine long standing traditions in depth and to undertake experimental innovation in the same area in which we had an interest."

The first concrete step toward a revision of the educational system—and the eventual establishment of Concordia Senior College, an upper division institution in Fort Wayne, Indiana—came at the annual convention of the synod held in 1944 in Saginaw, Michigan. At that time, the Board for Higher Education was "requested to make further studies regarding the advisability of changing over to a four-year college course in preparation for entrance upon a three-year course in theology in St. Louis" (Evangelical Lutheran Synod of Missouri, Ohio, and Other States, 1944, p. 492). As a first step in conducting the necessary studies, Neeb was employed in January 1945 as executive secretary for the board. "Prior to that time, individual Board members had explored and toyed with the general considerations involved"; following Neeb's employment, "the examination of these alternative possibilities and, in fact, the generation of them, accelerated very sharply" (Neeb, 1968a).

By 1946, the educational system had grown from the original seminary and preparatory school to a seminary, two teachers colleges, ten junior colleges with local affiliated high schools, and a number of Lutheran high schools not directly affiliated with any one of the junior colleges, although only one-half of the students in the junior colleges were ministerial students. Between 1944 and

1947, eighteen separate proposals for the restructuring of this system were submitted to the Board for Higher Education; yet, "before any decision could be made as to how the Church's college-level ministerial education should be operated, it was necessary to re-state, re-define, and re-investigate the validity of the objectives of total ministerial training by the Lutheran Church at both the college and the seminary level" (Lutheran Church—Missouri Synod, 1950, p. 213).

The feeling that "any changes in the present program could have value only to the extent that they might improve or expand the Church's ability to preach, teach, and apply the Gospel" led, at the 1947 convention, to consideration and passage of a new document, "The Objectives of Ministerial Training," which had been prepared by Neeb and members of the board during the preceding year. This document outlined the goals to be sought in any redefinition of the system: Students were to be provided with doctrinal knowledge, the means to attain a spiritually dominated personality, a Christian interpretation of basic subject matter, an appreciation of the minister's function, and personal skills. These goals were predicated upon the assumptions that the ultimate objective was the preparation of ministers, that ministerial education differed from general Christian education, and that both were distinctly different from secular education. "A School which adopts a dual objective and serves a student body in which a majority registers for general Christian education cannot at the same time," the board stated, "put its ministerial training program in anything but a second place" (Evangelical Lutheran Synod of Missouri, Ohio, and Other States, 1947, p. 170).

Thus, each of the eighteen reorganization proposals was viewed in terms not only of the ultimate structure of the educational system but also of its effect on the ability of the system to provide an educated, committed ministry. Basically, the proposals fell into three categories: those to establish a separate two- or four-year institution to provide the education required between the end of junior college and the start of seminary work, assuming that the seminary would require a baccalaureate degree for admission; those to attach two years of education to one or more of the existing junior colleges; and those to subsidize students' upper division education at another institution. Obviously, the third alternative was unsatisfactory since it would remove ministerial students from the synodical system of education for two years; it was discarded before the other proposals were examined in detail (Evangelical Lutheran Synod of Missouri, Ohio, and Other States, 1947, p. 178).

Creation of a new college, whether two or four years in length, was seen as by far the most expensive alternative; yet, "the possibility of achieving conditions in which the vital objectives of ministerial training may be readily reached may well make the most costly plan also the most desirable one." A decision to adapt one of the existing junior colleges, while less expensive, would necessitate additional land acquisition and construction and might lead to problems in the transfer of students to a new institution, the reassignment of faculty, and the securing of accreditation. Moreover, a decision to eliminate the nonministerial education programs at any given junior college—necessitated by the desire to have the new institution concerned solely with preprofessional ministerial students—could well lead to great dissatisfaction on the part of the local Lutheran constituency, whose support was necessary to the successful operation of any educational institution (Evangelical Lutheran Synod of Missouri, Ohio, and Other States, 1947, pp. 183–185).

In view of this potential local pressure, one of the recommendations of the board, ultimately adopted by the synod, was "that the present Junior College system be maintained." The board also reported that "earnest efforts to agree on the propriety of selecting any one of the proposed plans . . . revealed a wide divergence of opinion; however, after an objective discussion of the premises offered and of the relative merits of the various plans, the Advisory Council (College and Seminary presidents) concurred with your Board in the following Recommendations: That Synod establish a Senior College as an additional unit in the professional training of ministerial students." The board then proceeded to define a senior college as an institution "on the level of the junior and senior years of the American college system." Finally, the board was instructed to undertake studies regarding the location, curriculum,

and plant requirements for the new senior college (Evangelical Lutheran Synod of Missouri, Ohio, and Other States, 1947, pp. 200,
201).

Between 1947 and 1950, the next regularly scheduled synodical convention, discussion and planning for the new institution
proceeded under the direction of the executive secretary of the
board. The 1947 resolutions had "approved the idea that the Synod
would establish a senior college and that it would be an additional
unit, but how or on what terms were wide open in 1947" (Neeb,
1968a). During these three years, the executive secretary traveled
throughout the country to attend the thirty-six regional synods and
to discuss the plans for the new institution with local educational
and religious leaders. Concurrently, planning for the restructuring
of the entire educational system continued, leading in 1953 to the
approval of the new two-year upper division college at Fort Wayne.

By 1950, the specific aims and governing structure of the
new senior college had been determined, although a location was
still to be chosen. Conservative elements within the synod, however,
had mounted a campaign to reverse the 1947 decision to create a
separate, upper division institution. Thus, the primary resolutions
of the 1950 convention were designed to reinforce the 1947 resolution: "Resolved, That we proceed to carry out our resolutions of
1947 to establish a Senior College in accordance with the proposals
submitted to us at this time by our Board for Higher Education"
and that $2,750,000 be allocated for construction of the new cam-
pus when a location was finally decided upon. In addition, a Committee of 99 was appointed, including the president of each of the
thirty-six regional synods, parish clergy, and representatives of other
specific divisions of clergy and laymen, to assist the board in locating a site for the senior college (Lutheran Church—Missouri Synod,
1950, pp. 219–221, 225, 226–229, 230–234, 240–251)'.

The Committee of 99 met at the board offices in St. Louis
in January 1952 and recommended that the senior college be located in either the Chicago or the Milwaukee suburban areas primarily because of the geographical distribution throughout the nation of both the potential student body and the existing junior colleges. On November 18, 1952, an option was placed on a 126-acre

site northwest of Chicago, giving the impression that this would be the location of the new institution. Yet, before the next convention began on June 17, 1953, "an unsolicited offer was made by the Indiana Technical College of Fort Wayne to purchase our Concordia College at Fort Wayne." After careful consideration of all alternatives—and the assurance that another location within Fort Wayne could be found for a new institution—the synodical convention decided to abandon plans for the senior college in Chicago and to plan instead for its development in Fort Wayne (Lutheran Church —Missouri Synod, 1953, pp. 131, 132, 177).

The reasoning behind this decision provides an interesting insight into the factors which affected many of the decisions taken by the Board for Higher Education. Although the synod was seen by others as "a notable example of generosity in the financing of colleges" and "the Church [was] ready to provide the financial support necessary to carry out the program" of education which it had approved (Pattillo and MacKenzie, 1966, pp. 45, 259), the opportunity to receive $1 million for "the oldest existing campus" and the one in which "the Board for Higher Education had done . . . the least rehabilitating" could not be resisted by the synod (Neeb, 1968a). In addition the board exercised complete control over any major decisions relating to the individual campuses—despite the existence of a local board for each institution—and was "clearly the most influential factor in achieving the goal of the Church in higher education" (Pattillo and MacKenzie, 1966, p. 249). Thus, despite "opposition to the sale of the Junior College [which] was so pronounced that there were local groups who came to the convention [in 1953] with the purpose of stopping the sale," the board was able to secure approval from the synod for the sale (Neeb, 1968a).

In one sense, however, the board did acquiesce to the local constituency. The decision to sell the old campus did not necessarily mean that the new senior college would be located in Fort Wayne, even though Fort Wayne possessed many of the geographical advantages attributed to Chicago and Milwaukee. The sale of the old Fort Wayne institution was ultimately justified on grounds which were not unrelated to the new senior college, particularly the long-term costs of renovation of the old Fort Wayne campus and the high cost of contiguous improved property needed for expansion. Yet, mindful "that the discontinuance of the use of any campus, even when such a move is fully justified in every way, stirs feelings of regret" (Lutheran Church—Missouri Synod, 1956, p. 16), the synod, according to Neeb, made "a sort of trade" with the local board and constituency of Fort Wayne: the old institution for the new (1968a). With this compromise, events moved quickly. A new local board for the new institution, Concordia Senior College, was created; on April 9, 1954, Neeb was appointed the first president, and on January 31, 1955, he left the board to assume his new position. Finally, in September 1957, Concordia Senior College received its first class of 193 students, all of them, appropriately enough, graduates of one of the ten synod junior colleges, which had been reorganized to act as feeder institutions for the senior college, which itself fed the seminary in St. Louis.

Thus, in 1957, Concordia Senior College became the third upper division institution in the United States, although the first, College of the Pacific, had reverted to its four-year status six years earlier (see Chapter Four), leaving only Concordia and the New School Senior College in operation. These three institutions had each developed in response to a distinct set of local circumstances; yet, each in its own way reflected concern over the appropriate structure of a baccalaureate degree program. In each case, as at the University of Chicago, decisions had been reached which, if nothing else, determined that the point between the sophomore and junior years was a logical and convenient place to divide the baccalaureate degree.

In addition, each of these institutions reflected, to a varying degree, the influence of the German university concept on American colleges and universities. This influence is most clearly seen in the case of Concordia, which created a senior college because, although it possessed a complete preparatory (gymnasial) system of education, its university level, consisting only of the theological seminary, required two additional years in order to parallel the common American pattern. Similarly, the existence of one portion of a university at the New School and the need to create a base for this program led to the decision to offer undergraduate work; yet, only the last half of the baccalaureate was begun, in part because only this portion could be justified in terms of past offerings, which were seen as university rather than as secondary, or preparatory, in nature.

Finally, the decisions taken at Chicago, Pacific, and the New School in the 1940's mark the end of one major chapter in the history of upper division institutions in the United States. Prior to 1950, consideration of basic educational questions—such as the appropriate structure of a baccalaureate program, the distinction between university and nonuniversity work, and the best point at which to divide the baccalaureate experience among several levels of institutions—led to the suggestion of alternate organizational patterns, one of which was the upper division institution. Following 1950, the existence of rapidly growing systems of public junior colleges—themselves an answer to many of the questions which had led to the first upper division institutions—made consideration of alternate patterns of organization extremely difficult. Given the two-year junior colleges and a growing demand for more baccalaureate degrees, planners turned to new questions involving the best way to provide for the industrial and educational needs of their communities. In several instances, answers to these new questions pointed to the same organizational pattern arrived at by those considering the earlier questions in Stockton, New York, and Chicago: the upper division college.

Four

&&&&&&&&&&&&&&&&&&&&&&&&&

A Time to Question

&&&&&&&&&&&&&&&&&&&&&&&&&

The 1940's witnessed the creation of a new upper division college at the New School, the "relocation" of the baccalaureate degree at the University of Chicago, and the initial steps in the restructuring of the educational system of the Lutheran Church—Missouri Synod, which led to the creation of Concordia Senior College. During the 1950's, two experimental programs—at Chicago and at the College of the Pacific—were brought to an end, while the program at the New School was seriously threatened. Concurrently, educators in Florida, New York, and Michigan took the first steps toward the establishment of new upper division institutions.

During the 1940's, many changes had taken place at the College of the Pacific and its "lower division," Stockton Junior College (see Chapter Two). In 1942, Robert E. Burns, a graduate of the college and its registrar for seven years, became assistant to President Tully Knoles; in 1946, he succeeded to the presidency upon Knoles's retirement and elevation to the position of chancellor. Concurrently, there were many personnel changes at the junior college. Dwayne Orton left as principal in 1942; following a succession of several principals over the next few years, Leon P. Minear was appointed president of the college—now known as Stockton College—in 1949. The change in name had accompanied the expansion of the junior college to a four-year community college in May 1948 as part of the reorganized six-four-four plan authorized by the Stockton Board of Education on March 24, 1944 (Stockton Board of Education, 1941–1945).

The Second World War had also affected both institutions, particularly in terms of enrollment. Enrollment at the junior college, which had risen to a high of 2,620 in the fall of 1941, fell to 1,224 during the 1942–1943 academic year, its lowest since 1937–1938. Following the war, enrollment rapidly rose again at both institutions, creating a strain on the shared facilities of the College of the Pacific. The Stockton school board secured a number of temporary buildings from the federal government—buildings which had been constructed during the war to house the Navy V-12 program, in which both institutions had participated—and, after renovation, opened them in 1948 for use as classrooms, student union, library, gymnasium, and cafeteria. Although the use of these buildings removed much of the pressure on facilities—pressure increased by the junior college expansion to a four-year program—both the decision to tie the junior college more closely than previously to the public school system through the adoption of the six-four-four plan and the related decision to acquire separate buildings for the junior college created a new strain on the relations between it and the College of the Pacific.

Thus, by 1949, the year of Minear's appointment as president of Stockton College, the two institutions had begun to drift apart, even though Stockton College still rented some of its facilities from the College of the Pacific. The expansion of the vocational education offerings at Stockton College had led for the first time to the employment of many faculty members who were not also associated with the College of the Pacific; furthermore, as time progressed, many of the original faculty departed, being replaced at both institutions with new personnel who felt loyalty neither to the shared campus nor to the working arrangements instituted in 1935–1936. Gradually, as a result of all these factors, Stockton College began to develop an identity of its own, separate from the College of the Pacific, as well as its own buildings, course offerings, and faculty.

The two institutions still maintained a joint student body and joint participation in many student activities, including the athletic teams. On January 20, 1950, however, Knoles, acting on behalf of Burns, who was ill, reported that "it is a determination of the President of Stockton College to make Stockton College increasingly a unit and as a result a change in the Student Body Organization is being made." After that, each institution had its own student organization, although students in one institution had the opportunity to join the other student organization if their schedules required that they participate in activities on the other campus. As he surveyed the steadily worsening relations between the two institutions—and noted that "increasingly classes are being moved to the Stockton College campus and the tendency is to leave on this campus those classes which are expensive to operate"—Knoles suggested that the board consider the possibility of reinstating a full four-year program at the College of the Pacific (College of the Pacific, 1949–1955, p. 325).

At the March 28 meeting of the board, both Burns and Knoles reported on the relationship with Stockton College and presented the pros and cons of reestablishing a lower division at Pacific. Knoles felt that "relations between the two schools had reached a place where cooperation is almost impossible" (College of the Pacific, 1949–1955, p. 329), a situation which Burns attributed to "a cantankerous school board with a new and difficult administrator" and to the fact that "academic cooperation . . . is coming to a point where there is little more than a rental of our facilities." Yet, the income to the College of the Pacific from this rental in the fall of 1949 amounted to over $47,000, and Stockton College had already informed Burns that it would require even more space during the coming academic year. Burns's recommendation, which was accepted, was "that we sit tight, but watch the situation very carefully" (Burns, 1950a, p. 5).

Both Knoles and Burns agreed that the present structure, under which the College of the Pacific had no responsibility for the lower division offerings, had several advantages, including the income from rental, the savings in personnel and laboratory costs, and the large number of students, drawn to a tuition-free institution, from which to choose their junior class. Yet, both felt that the "clashes with the administration of Stockton College and the School Board" made operation under these conditions increasingly difficult; moreover, despite the rental payments, the college was not compensated for the increased wear and tear on buildings and equipment. Finally, although the addition of a lower division would require the employment of from twenty-one to twenty-six additional faculty and administrative personnel, depending on the size of the class admitted, and the purchase of equipment and the provision of additional scholarships, Burns (1950a) computed that the income from tuition would exceed these expenses by $3,000 a year for a lower division of 200 students and by $68,000 a year for a lower division of 400 students.

Although no mention had been made of these discussions to the Stockton school board, that board also realized that relations were deteriorating. On May 4, 1950, it requested a joint meeting with the Board of Trustees of the College of the Pacific "in the interest of promoting a better understanding between the two colleges" (Stockton Board of Education, 1949–1951, p. 308). Nonetheless, the Stockton board proceeded with its own plans to replace the temporary government buildings into which it had moved after the war with a new group of permanent facilities on its own campus. On June 13, the Stockton Board of Education announced the start of construction of a new library building, and on July 18, a new art building was approved. Overshadowing both these events, however, was the fact that on June 25, 1950, the Korean War began.

Burns later stated that "if the Korean War hadn't come along, I suspect we might still be an upper-division–graduate institution" (1968). Although this is probably an overstatement, the war did have great effects upon both institutions. Almost immediately, the Army petitioned the College of the Pacific to establish ROTC classes; on October 20, Burns noted that "the draft will probably begin to make heavy inroads in February [1951] and conscription is also a probability" (College of the Pacific, 1949–1955, p. 363). Deciding on November 10, 1950, that an ROTC program, which would "protect" students during their years in college, was preferable to the uncertainties of the draft, the board approved the establishment of an ROTC unit on the campus.

The war also had an adverse effect on Stockton College; 423 students were drafted during the first six months of the conflict. Since junior colleges could not offer ROTC—and since the break between the junior college and the upper division offered a logical point at which to draft men—there was an increased fear, according to Burns, that the College of the Pacific would not continue to receive an adequate number of transfer students from the junior colleges of the state. Moreover, junior college students who were tempted to enlist at the end of their sophomore year might not make the same choice if they were enrolled in a four-year institution. Thus, Burns saw the outbreak of war as yet another reason to consider reestablishment of a lower division at Pacific (1968).

Still officially unaware of the reconsideration at Pacific of its structure, the Stockton school board, on October 10, 1950, approved a rental contract for $100,000 for the following academic year; ten days later, however, Burns (1950b, p. 5) made another report to his own board on "the lower division problem which is probably the most serious problem to be faced in years." Two new difficulties had recently arisen, one in connection with athletics and the other with accreditation. Burns reported that the American Chemical Society had refused to accredit the Pacific program since, in the words of the society, "the present organization of the College of the Pacific cannot permit the Department of Chemistry to retain proper control over the caliber and scope of the lower level courses and training." In addition, Burns had just received notification that all intercollegiate athletic events with Pacific had been canceled because of pressure on other colleges from the Pacific Coast Conference, which had expelled the college for continuing to allow sophomores from Stockton College to participate on its teams (p. 6).

Burns believed that the problems with the American Chemical Society—and anticipated problems with Phi Beta Kappa and the engineering accrediting body—could be solved only through addition of a lower division or at least through addition of lower division courses in those areas in which the college wished subject-matter accreditation. With respect to the ruling of the Pacific Coast Conference, Burns felt that the options were basically the same: continue the situation as it was, with the resulting loss of intercollegiate athletics; organize a lower division from which to draw sophomore athletes, while continuing "to rent any facilities that are left to Stockton College on about the same basis as before"; or organize a sophomore class or series of classes to permit athletes to register at Pacific. Although Burns closed the October 20 board meeting with the statement that he favored a lower division, he once again recommended that the board "go slow," particularly since the meeting with the Stockton Board of Education requested by that body the previous May was scheduled to be held within the next three weeks (College of the Pacific, 1949–1955, pp. 359, 361; Burns, 1950b, p. 5).

The joint meeting was held November 8, 1950. Representatives of the College of the Pacific, including Burns, Knoles, and four trustees, presented a résumé of the difficulties the college faced under the present administrative arrangement. Burns stated that Pacific would like to establish "a pilot lower division as sort of a model, highly selective group" consisting of 300 students, the number withdrawn from the Pacific campus over the past year as Stockton College continued to move into its new buildings. The same rental agreements for the same amount of space would continue to be in effect, Stockton College students could continue to use Pacific dormitories and dining facilities, and an attempt would be made to enroll thirteenth- and fourteenth-year Stockton College students in the new ROTC program (College of the Pacific, 1949–1955).

The Stockton board, although taking no formal action, gave tacit approval to the proposals (Burns, 1968). At the November meeting of the College of the Pacific board, held two days after the joint meeting, the trustees decided to move ahead with plans to institute a lower division program for 300 students. Burns was asked to formulate specific plans for the program and to announce the decision of the board. The following issue of the student newspaper, *Pacific Weekly* (1950, p. 1), announced that "COP Adds Frosh, Sophs"; the reasons, cited from the board discussions, were given as the desire to meet "educational standardizing requirements," the requirements of athletic conferences, and the requirements of ROTC, and the desire to serve a larger (Methodist) constituency. The paper also noted the decision to limit enrollment to 300 "to allow junior college use of facilities."

For some reason, the Stockton school board made no formal comment on the new arrangements until June 28, 1951, seven months after the decision had been made and a full month after the new Pacific catalogue announced that "with the fall class of 1951 the College will reinstitute its lower division" (College of the Pacific, 1951, p. 23). In the interim, the Stockton board moved ahead with its own plans to form an independent band (necessitated by the January 1950 decision to divide the student bodies of the two institutions) and to choose new school colors for Stockton College. Concurrently, Burns carried out the request of the board to plan for the new lower division, announcing on March 11, 1951, that the plans were complete and that 387 inquiries had been received to date. Finally, in the fall of 1951, the new lower division was opened with an enrollment of 202 freshmen and 68 sophomores.

One reason for the failure of the Stockton board to make formal comment on the new arrangements was its desire, despite the establishment of the lower division at Pacific, to continue to rent space on the Pacific campus and to avoid aggravating an already complicated situation; furthermore, insofar as Stockton College was concerned, there had been no loss except for a possible drain of students who could afford the Pacific tuition. The new rental contract was approved on August 1, 1951; in fact, the junior college continued to rent facilities from the College of the Pacific for several years, reducing its needs in stages as its new campus (across the street from the College of the Pacific) was gradually completed. At the same time, the College of the Pacific, having survived the depression through its arrangement with the Stockton Board of Education, returned once again to its "great emphasis on the teaching function of the undergraduate years" (Burns, 1968).

Although the College of the Pacific experiment had come to an end, it had not failed, in any sense, because of an inherent weakness in the concept of an upper division institution, although this would not always be the case with other institutions. In Stockton, the initial plan had been developed as a cooperative venture between a public school board and a private institution; over the years, because of changing conditions and personnel, that cooperation had gradually lessened, increasing the stress on both institutions. Yet the public institution, with its broader base of support and of potential students and with a growing desire for an independent identity, did not react to these stresses in the same way or to the same degree as did the College of the Pacific. The Pacific reaction was due, in great measure, to the additional pressures brought to bear by outside forces—specifically accreditation bodies, athletic conferences, and the war—which would not or could not adjust their own requirements to the unique conditions on the Stockton campus.

The College of the Pacific had eventually discovered what many other experimental programs involving the structure of education had discovered: that a single institution, regardless of the degree to which it is internally satisfied with an organizational structure different from that of those institutions with which it interacts, cannot continue to operate under these conditions if the other institutions (or accrediting bodies or athletic conferences) do not make certain necessary adjustments. Thus, most experiments with six-four-four, including those at Pasadena and, eventually, in Stockton, were abandoned when difficulties arose in providing transfers for their students to and from other, more traditional systems of education. In the same manner, the Lutheran Church—Missouri Synod system was finally modified, at least to the extent that the major educational divisions—high school, college (although two separate units), and graduate school—and the appropriate degrees were brought into line with the existing American pattern, when the system, partially through the influence of the Second World War, was forced into greater interaction with other systems than it had previously experienced. Likewise, in 1953, the University of Chicago reversed its earlier decision on the relocation of the baccalaureate and brought its own degree offerings and structure back into line with the overwhelming majority of American institutions of higher education.

The Chicago College Plan, begun in 1931, entered its second phase in 1942 with the announcement by President Robert M. Hutchins that the University of Chicago would offer the baccalaureate degree following the sophomore year of college and was creating, in effect, a four-year junior college by combining the lower division college with the two final years at the university high school (see Chapters Two and Three). Hutchins left the university in 1951, after serving first as president and then as chancellor for twenty-two years, and was replaced by Chancellor Lawrence A. Kimpton. One of Kimpton's first actions as chancellor was to review the success and operation of the Chicago College Plan.

The results of Kimpton's review were both encouraging and disheartening. On the bright side, the university discovered through extensive study of graduate record examinations that "the average graduate of the College [after the sophomore year] is able to demonstrate a superior achievement in at least two 'fields of study' and . . . the strongest graduates of the College, who are most apt to undertake graduate study, exhibit . . . 'exceptional achievement.' " Furthermore, a representative group of college "seniors" was found to be equal to the national average on most general tests and better than this average on advanced tests (Bloom and Ward, 1952, pp. 462–464, 466).

On the other hand, the average student in the college was no longer able to complete the two-year college baccalaureate in two years; by 1951, the average student stay was three full years. Furthermore, the vast majority of students entering the Chicago program did so after completion of a regular four-year high school, rather than at the start of the junior year of high school as Hutchins had originally intended. Students were also not receiving the advantages of a unified four-year arts curriculum, grades eleven through fourteen, as had been the initial idea (Bloom and Ward, 1952); in fact, the official announcement of the change, recognizing the nature of the entering students and the time in which the degree was normally completed, spoke not of requiring two additional years for the new baccalaureate (as would have been appropriate with respect to the official position of the university) but of adding one additional year of study to that normally required by the students themselves.

The "new" baccalaureate plan was put into effect in the fall of 1953; during that year, entering students were given the option of enrolling under either the old or the new program of studies. By the fall of 1954, however, all admissions were to the four-year, college-level baccalaureate, now similar in structure, if not in course content or curricular organization, to the traditional four-year American college. Provision was still made for individual students qualified to begin their college education after their sophomore year in high school, but for all practical purposes, the Chicago College experiment had come to an end. Despite university publicity that this was but the third step in a natural progression, many American educators agreed with the analysis of R. H. Eckelberry (1953, p. 388), editor of *The Journal of Higher Education,* who viewed the move as "a retreat from the extreme position that general and special education are separate and distinct, that one is the job of the undergraduate college and the other that of the graduate professional school, and that one must be completed (so far as formal schooling is concerned) before the other is begun."

By 1953, the experimental programs at both the College of the Pacific and the University of Chicago had been ended, and the two institutions had redesigned their programs and structures to conform to those in the typical American college. By that same date, planning for the new Concordia Senior College had been mostly completed, although the institution would not open for another four years. As of 1953, the only upper division program remaining in operation was that at the New School in New York, begun nearly a decade earlier during the presidency of Alvin Johnson, who retired in 1945 (see Chapter Three). The New School program had never achieved a substantial enrollment—by 1958, after fourteen years in operation, it had awarded 320 baccalaureate degrees—and, during the 1950's, it too faced the threat of being expanded to a four-year collegiate program.

The baccalaureate program at the New School was always intended to be a "sideline rather than the center of our activities"; there is some doubt, however, that the program would have been approved by the State Education Department in 1944 if it had realized the extent to which this statement would be true. A detailed self-study, prepared in 1952 after the institution had failed in a 1948 attempt to receive accreditation from the Middle States Association of Colleges and Universities, noted that "this new departure [the upper division baccalaureate program], undertaken to serve the needs of returning service men and women under the G. I. program and also to increase the income of the School, has apparently not affected the curriculum of the School to any marked degree" (Swift, 1952, p. II-37)`.

The 1948 attempt at accreditation, undertaken by the new president, Bryn J. Hovde, had failed for a number of reasons, several of them directly related to the baccalaureate program. According to the Middle States Association report, cited in another self-study prepared in 1958, administration of the undergraduate program—which did not even have its own dean—was inadequate, as were library facilities, and there were too few full-time faculty members and too much reliance on "open courses [for both credit and noncredit students] as integral parts of the B.A. program." The report was especially critical of the mixture of students—a natural outcome of the decision not to initiate special courses for baccalaureate students—and also noted that preparation, participation, and self-evaluation on the part of faculty, students, and administration of the New School was inadequate (McGrath, 1958, p. 14).

In 1950, with Hovde's retirement, Hans Simons was appointed president of the New School. With the advice of some former members of the accreditation team, Simons moved to correct some of the faults which they had noted, although his ultimate purpose was not necessarily to reapply for accreditation. On the contrary, Simons (1968)` did not see accreditation as an urgent matter as long as graduates of the New School were being accepted by accredited institutions for graduate study as, in fact, they were. During the academic year 1955–1956, for example, 318 students were enrolled for baccalaureate credit, of which ninety-one were fully matriculated for the degree. Of the 1956 graduating class of fifteen, twelve had gone on to do graduate work at seven institutions, including Columbia University, New York University, City College, and the University of Chicago, as well as the New School itself.

In 1954, construction was begun on new buildings for the New School, and by the fall of 1956, the first building was ready to be occupied. According to Simons (1968)—who had stated in 1944 that one purpose of the baccalaureate program was "to underpin the structure of the Graduate Faculty"—the opening of the new buildings offered an opportunity to complete the underpinning of the graduate programs by creating an integrated four-year college for adults and unusually mature and independent high school graduates. The new college would combine day and evening classes, required and optional courses, and a multitude of educational approaches designed to broaden the student's education within the larger "campus" of New York City.

Simons' first step, in early 1957, was to consult informally with representatives of the State Education Department, which, according to Simons (1957a), "was ready to support any preliminary inquiries concerned with additional facilities for college education." Concurrently, Simons consulted with the New School deans, members of the graduate faculty, and, on June 25, 1957, with the Educational Policy Committee of the Board of Trustees, to which he explained his tentative plans to provide "a firmer anchor in a four-year curriculum" for the New School program (Simons, 1957b). The committee agreed that the project was feasible and desirable and authorized Simons to continue his investigations. On August 5, Simons sent a copy of his tentative plans to Ewald B. Nyquist, deputy commissioner of education in Albany; Nyquist's reply called the plans "the most exciting curricular proposal I have seen in some time and a worthy sharp departure from the usual ones which come to my attention." "You may accept this letter," Nyquist (1957) continued, "as official encouragement from the Department for its accomplishment."

Following these initial indications of support, Simons began a lengthy series of consultations. Representatives of the Fund for the Advancement of Education, the Rockefeller Foundation, and the Kellogg Foundation were approached for financial support. Educational considerations were discussed, in person and by letter, with educators throughout the country and in England, with members of the New School faculty, administration, and student body, and with students and faculty from other New York City institutions, both secondary and collegiate. Reaction from the Fund for the Advancement of Education was definitely positive, and Simons was encouraged to submit a formal proposal before the end of the year (1957); nonetheless, Simons (1957a) reported to the board in November 1957 that "expert opinion is divided on the educational merits of the plan as it now stands."

Opinion was also divided within the New School itself. Dean Arthur Swift (1957) felt "the plan an excellent one, capable of being effectuated and meeting a combination of circumstances which make it decidedly timely." Other observers seriously questioned the financial aspects of the program, although Swift strongly urged that budget "not be the determining factor in the decision" and Hans Staudinger (1957), dean of the graduate faculty, felt that "rightly budgeted, the Day College would be, in the long run, not a risk but an income producer."

By the beginning of 1958, the arguments on both sides were clearly drawn. Those in favor of the proposal, including Simons and most of his administrative staff, felt that the new program, in addition to making a valuable educational contribution, would make better use of the new facilities than was now possible with the emphasis on evening studies. Those opposed—or with reservations—including Earl J. McGrath, author of a study prepared for the New School in late 1957, were fearful that the financial burden would be too great and that "as the New School becomes more conventional . . . the original purpose of providing a broad education for a selected group of adult citizens would by force of circumstances be obscured" (1958, p. 20). A third group, including

Johnson (1958), felt that "such a college alone [designed to produce a liberally educated man] would be worth the serious effort
the New School would have to make in its launching and operation" but that "we seem often to be somewhat hazy about [what]
the educational character of such an institution" would be.

According to Simons (1968), the Board of Trustees hesi-
tated to support such a radical departure from the New School
tradition, even though the tradition was to be nontraditional; moreover, the board was concerned about financing, even though the
Fund for the Advancement of Education had informally agreed to
underwrite the anticipated deficit. On January 20, 1958, Simons
(1958b) presented a report to the Educational Policy Committee
designed to answer any outstanding questions regarding the timing,
staffing, or financing of the proposed day college; on March 3, the
committee finally recommended action and authorized a formal request to the fund for a minimum of $500,000 over two years "to
guarantee the New School against its incurring any financial losses
or additional financial burdens from the project" (Simons, 1958a).
Yet at the March 4 meeting of the full board, the final plan "failed
to find the unanimous support of the trustees" (New School, 1960,
p. xii); although a majority of the board had voted in favor of
the proposals, as Simons (1968) stated, such an important and far-
reaching move had been defeated for lack of virtual unanimity.

Thus, the proposal to modify the structure of the New
School upper division institution failed, and the senior college continued to operate for juniors and seniors only. Neither the reasons
given for making the change nor those for refusing it were based
on consideration of the strengths or weaknesses inherent in the existing upper division organization. Simons wanted a full four-year
program to underpin his graduate work; a major consideration was
that the program should be day-time to make better use of existing
facilities and, as a day-time program, would be aimed at a different
student group, one less likely to have had previous college experience. For those opposed to the day college proposal, fear of an influx of adolescents, coupled with very real concerns about financing,
eventually caused the proposal to be defeated.

Five

❧❧❧❧❧❧❧❧❧❧❧❧❧❧❧❧❧❧❧❧❧❧❧❧❧

A Time to Create

❧❧❧❧❧❧❧❧❧❧❧❧❧❧❧❧❧❧❧❧❧❧❧❧❧

In 1953, following the termination of the Chicago experiment, the New School College was the only existing upper division institution. By 1958, however, two new institutions had begun operation, and planning was under way for three more. One of those institutions already in operation was Concordia Senior College in Fort Wayne, Indiana; the other, which opened in 1956, was Flint College, the first unit of the University of Michigan to offer degrees away from the main Ann Arbor campus.

Although the University of Michigan had considered establishing undergraduate programs in several Michigan cities including Flint during the late 1940's, the Flint drive to secure a four-year institution began in earnest in mid-1950, in large measure because of the efforts of Michael Gorman, then editor of the *Flint Journal*

(Cummings, 1968; Totten, 1968). Initial impetus came from approval of a $7 million bond issue in Flint on June 6, 1950, of which $1.5 million was to be used for construction of new buildings at the local junior college; concurrently Charles Stewart Mott—one of the founders of General Motors, president of the Mott Foundation, and a noted Flint philanthropist—stated that the foundation stood ready to provide $1 million toward construction of a four-year college for Flint (*Flint Journal,* 1950a, 1950b). Three days later, at the urging of Gorman, University of Michigan President Herbert Reuthven (a close personal friend), Provost James Adams, and several members of the University of Michigan Board of Regents, a citizens' committee was established; among the twelve members were Gorman, Frank Manley of the foundation staff, J. A. Anderson of General Motors A. C. Sparkplug Division in Flint, Everett A. Cummings, president of a local bank and member of the Flint Board of Education, and W. Fred Totten, president of Flint Junior College. At its first meeting, held June 23, 1950, the Flint Citizens' Committee (1952, p. 2) decided that "a complete study should be made of the question of the four-year college for Flint."

At some point before January 19, 1951, Gorman sent a detailed memorandum to Adams outlining some of the thinking of the Flint committee. Noting that enrollment at the Ann Arbor campus was growing rapidly and that "Flint is substantially the largest community in Michigan without a four-year college," Gorman discussed the required capital and operating costs, projected enrollment, and sources of support for a new institution in Flint; among the latter was listed $1.7 million which the Board of Education had on hand "for a new Junior College." "Flint, presumably, is ready to go either on its own or with some sponsorship," Gorman (n.d.) concluded. "If the University is confronted with a problem of size, and development of outposts then is a reasonable solution, its position of educational leadership in the State advises proceeding promptly." Adams, in a letter dated February 5, promised to bring the matter to the Board of Regents at their next meeting.

Adams "reported on the proposal to expand Flint Junior College under the general supervision of the University" at the February 15 meeting of the Board of Regents, who "requested that a full report of a study to be made concerning these recommendations be submitted." At the March board meeting, Adams reported that the study, under the direction of Algo D. Henderson, professor of education at the university, was progressing smoothly, and the regents requested "that the study include the question of the basic policy of whether the University should establish branch colleges in the state" (University of Michigan, 1951, pp. 1226, 1254).

The introduction of the general question of branch campuses complicated Henderson's consideration of the Flint situation. At the outset, neither the university nor the Flint representatives had defined the nature of the institution to be considered, although the regents had assumed in February that future discussions would be centered around a proposal to expand the local junior college "under the general supervision of the University." Now, in the midst of his appraisal of the specific possibilities for a branch in Flint, Henderson was asked to comment on the more general and basic question of whether any branch campuses should be established by the university.

The resulting report, completed in April, was understandably confused. After a general survey of the experiences of other states with branch campuses, Henderson (1951, pp. 4–7, 10) reported that "the University of Michigan probably cannot meet the future demands for its services on a single campus" and concluded that there was no reason why the university should not establish additional units in other locations where the local situation also indicated a need for them. A brief survey of the state showed that Flint was the only community which might demonstrate such a need, although "it seems probable that Flint could successfully establish and operate a public college of its own." Finally, assuming that a unit of the university might be established in Flint, Henderson concluded that it "should be a college of the University with its own faculty and program designed to meet the needs of the Flint area" and neither "a step-child of the University, nor a collection of extension branches of departments within the University."

On May 19, the regents deferred action on the Henderson report. What Henderson had discovered was that branch campuses were worthwhile if done well; that there was a need for them in terms of enrollment at Ann Arbor but not in terms of the educational needs of most communities in Michigan; that Flint would benefit from a branch campus but would also benefit from the establishment of its own institution. Moreover, Henderson had not addressed himself to the ultimate relations between such a branch, if established, and the existing junior college, except to note as a general rule that "inasmuch as the public junior colleges have only a limited program, the state should be alert to provide four-year colleges in regions where the population warrants and where private institutions or other public colleges do not sufficiently take care of the needs" (Henderson, 1951, p. 9).

During the summer of 1951—while action on Henderson's report was still pending—Marvin Niehuss was appointed to replace Adams as provost of the university and, on September 14, received a letter from Anderson (1951), chairman of the Flint College Committee, reminding him "that we have some unfinished business in regard to possible participation of the University of Michigan in the operation of a four-year college in Flint." Niehuss promised that the new president, Harlan Hatcher, would present the most recent Flint request for action to the Board of Regents at the earliest possible date. On January 18, 1952, Hatcher "reported informally on the progress made to date in discussion with representatives regarding the proposed relationship between the University and Flint Junior College" (University of Michigan, 1954, p. 274).

By this time, Hatcher and Niehuss had become aware of a shift in the Flint position; although no official statements had yet been made, Flint was no longer interested in any four-year arrangements but was leaning heavily toward some arrangement which would preserve the autonomy of the local junior college. In March, Hatcher asked Henderson to set up a joint committee with interested Flint citizens to refine the possibilities being discussed and to make recommendations for the regents; following several meetings with a group from Flint, including Cummings, Totten, Anderson, Manley, and George Gundry, chairman of the Flint Board of Education, Henderson (1952a) submitted his recommendations on May 20, 1952. The basic conclusion was that despite certain legal and financial difficulties which the Flint representatives had raised, "the

University would prefer to operate a single, integrated four-year unit" in Flint.

Henderson's recommendation was unacceptable to the Flint committee for several reasons. For one, the Flint Citizens' Committee, constituted in June 1950, had, on April 30, 1952, submitted its own recommendations (p. 4): "That the Board of Education officially confer with authorized representatives of the University of Michigan with a view to determining the nature and extent of the interest of the University of Michigan in the operation and administration of the third and fourth years of a four-year college program in Flint." The Flint committee had concluded "that the identity of Flint Junior College [should] be maintained," partially out of community pride for an institution which had been in operation for thirty years, partially to ensure the continued operation of a number of community and adult education programs which the community college offered, and partially because of financial considerations which made it advantageous to maintain the identity of the junior college (Cummings, 1968; Totten, 1968).

Henderson was aware of some of these factors, if not of the conclusions which would be reached; in fact, his May (1952a) report had outlined an alternative proposal which involved maintaining the legal identity of the junior college, although "the University should administer the whole of the program of the college, including the junior college division." The Flint reply to the Henderson proposals, delayed until October for "detailed study," recommended an alternate plan. "We believe it desirable that the Flint college program be separated into two distinct phases," the committee wrote, one of which would be the Flint Junior College and the other "the Senior College including the equivalent of the third and fourth year of the University of Michigan programs to be operated by the University." Two reasons were given for maintaining this separation: the availability of state aid for junior college programs and the existence of a trust fund, left to the junior college by W. S. Ballenger, which would "go elsewhere should Flint Junior College cease to exist" (Flint Board of Education, 1952).

The University of Michigan and the Flint community appear to have missed several opportunities to reach agreement during the early stages of the negotiations, particularly between May and October 1952. Although Henderson had recommended creation of "a single, integrated four-year unit" in Flint, he had listed a number of possible alternatives, including university administration of a program which would maintain the legal identity of the junior college. The Flint committee preferred a program "separated into two distinct phases"; yet, the needs for creating a bisected program as given by the committee would also have been met through Henderson's plan to maintain the legal identity of the existing college. The failure to reach agreement was based on a number of factors, including the differing perspectives of the university (statewide needs) and Flint (local needs and pride) officials; moreover, some of the Flint representatives felt "that Dr. Henderson's committee . . . was sort of set up to appease the Flint community" and that "the University wasn't seriously considering establishing a continuation of the University in Flint for two years" (Cummings, 1968).

The Flint proposals, viewed as a new alternative for discussion, were analyzed by Henderson (1952b) in a memorandum to Hatcher on November 18, 1952. Henderson saw at least five basic problems in the operation of independent institutions—the existence of separate administrations, the establishment of space utilization priorities, the definition of relations between extracurricular activities at the two institutions, the duplication of library, and the necessity for separate public relations—which would mitigate against acceptance of the Flint proposals. "Having made some analysis of these problems," Henderson reported, "the committee is proceeding to study the Flint proposal from the constructive viewpoint to see how the plan as proposed by Flint could be implemented and operated." At a meeting held the following week by Hatcher, Henderson, and Niehuss, the university decided to continue discussions with the Flint representatives to ascertain whether some mutually acceptable solution could be reached.

Discussions between the two groups continued through the early months of 1953, each discussion centering on defining the difficulties involved in meeting the Flint request for two separate institutions in terms of construction, faculty, maintenance of facilities, students, and administrative coordination (Henderson, 1953b).

Finally, on May 6, 1953, Henderson (1953a) submitted his final report to Hatcher. "Initially," he wrote, "the Flint Committee placed emphasis upon the funds available to finance a four-year college and upon their desire to have the University of Michigan establish in Flint an educational program similar in quality to that at Ann Arbor and to grant University degrees." Under these assumptions, the university had presented plans (May 1952) for a unified program, either incorporating the junior college into a new institution or maintaining its legal identity. Yet, "in October your committee was advised that the Flint Board desired to retain the Junior College and the University was asked to consider operating the upper two years."

Henderson then outlined the disadvantages of operating two separate institutions; in addition to the five reasons noted in his November 1952 memo, he added the disproportionately high costs of an upper division institution for the university, the prospects for "competition rather than cooperation" between the two institutions, and the fact that the university program "would be dependent for its students upon a junior program not under our control." Since "your committee has not been able to see the same merit in participating in a divided operation in Flint that we believed lay in either of our earlier proposals," Henderson recommended that the president "ask the Flint Board of Education to reconsider the possibility of having a four-year integrated college under the administration of either the Flint Board of Education or of the University." If this proposal were not accepted, Henderson then recommended "acceptance of the proposal from the Flint Board of Education as soon as a solution satisfactory to the University and to the Board of Education is found to the financial question." Hatcher acted upon only the first suggestion, which was refused, and conversations were suspended indefinitely.

The discussions lay dormant until, on December 8, 1954— more than eighteen months after the last formal communication— Cummings, now president of the Flint Board of Education, wrote to the Board of Regents suggesting that conversations be reopened. Cummings' letter was the culmination of one series of discussions as much as it was the beginning of another. Once again, as in 1950,

Gorman entered the picture to act as a catalyst (Niehusss, 1968; Cummings, 1968). "So many committees have been involved with negligible avail," wrote Gorman (1954), "that I felt someone with a sympathetic interest in both directions might make a contribution by informally seeking an area of potential accord." Gorman's contribution, made during November in a series of private meetings with Niehuss and Hatcher, was to outline a plan for the operation of two institutions in Flint which presented a satisfactory solution to the problems cited in Henderson's memo of May 1953 to Hatcher.

Gorman's suggestions, repeated in Cummings' letter to the board, centered on three points. To minimize the potential problems of precedence for the university, the university would take the position that it was willing, as a general rule, to offer faculty and administration for the third and fourth years only "in a community ready to supply buildings and maintenance" and to ensure adequate local support, both financial and in terms of students. Noting that enrollment at the university had reached record proportions—increasing the need for some branch offerings—and that enrollment at Flint Junior College had increased by 500 students during the last year alone—both a promise of adequate numbers of students and a reflection of "the possibility of a four-year college"—Gorman sensed "a new urgency" and was "convinced the matter has reached the stage where it is even more important to the University than it is to Flint." Finally, Gorman suggested that the request to the legislature for funds be made separately from the regular university budget, both to increase the effect of Flint efforts to lobby on its behalf and to stress its development as "an alternative for State help which might forestall the movement toward broad aid for Junior Colleges," which the university had previously resisted.

Obviously, Gorman's work was well done. On January 17, 1955, Hatcher wrote to the Board of Regents supporting Cummings' request and recommending that a formal agreement between the university and the Flint board be negotiated. Hatcher admitted that there were still many potential difficulties to be resolved but stressed the responsibility of the university to the state as a whole and the overwhelming support within the Flint community. "Is the University of Michigan a geographic fact or is it a mission, a program, a concept of education, a kingdom of the mind and of the spirit?" Hatcher asked rhetorically. "It is not geography," Hatcher (1955) concluded, "but purpose and accomplishment." At its January meeting, the Board of Regents instructed Hatcher to prepare the necessary plans and agreements.

From that point, events moved swiftly. A university planning committee, chaired by Professor Harold M. Dorr, was established in February, and Vice President (formerly Provost) Niehuss successfully presented the university case to the Committee on Ways and Means of the House of Representatives in early April. On April 13, the formal donation of $1 million by the Mott Foundation was made to the university, and one week later, the Flint community offered an additional $25,000 if needed. Another exchange of correspondence in late April secured the agreement "that facilities which are now available to the Junior College students would also be made available on an equal basis to the Senior College students, subject to programing and scheduling, without cost to the state" (Niehuss, 1955b; Cummings, 1955). Finally, on April 25, Niehuss (1955a) reported that complete agreement had been reached on all financial questions, including the fact that no state funds would be required for either construction or maintenance of facilities for 1,000 students but "only for operation of the educational program and for the building operating expenses."

Concurrently, Dorr's committee was at work and, in August 1955, presented its report on the academic and administrative organization of the new institution. Planning for Flint College, supported by a $37,000 preliminary appropriation from the legislature, continued throughout the winter in both Flint and Ann Arbor. Finally, on March 16, 1955, the Board of Regents formally declared its "intention to establish a Flint College of the University of Michigan and to declare that such college shall in all respects enjoy the legal status and prerogatives of other schools and colleges comprising the University" (University of Michigan, 1957, p. 951). The fourth upper division college in the nation had been created and was opened for classes in September 1956.

The decisions leading to the establishment of Flint College were greatly affected by local considerations within both Flint and the University of Michigan. Yet, despite these local considerations —which of necessity would vary from one community and situation to another—the pattern of events in Flint was typical of that followed later in the establishment of other upper division institutions. By the mid-1950's, many areas were beginning to experience or to anticipate increasing demand for higher education as a result of the postwar baby boom; by the same time, publicly supported systems of junior colleges were rapidly expanding and gave promise of providing increasing numbers of students with an opportunity for at least two years of college education. Given the existence of these junior colleges, educators were no longer concerned with theoretical or educational questions concerning the existing organizational structure. Rather, when need for increased baccalaureate education was determined—because of specific industrial demands or because of sheer numbers of students—planners acknowledged the existence of junior colleges and investigated ways of providing baccalaureate education with the least financial and academic duplication of effort. In Flint, as in other communities during the late 1950's and the early 1960's, planners saw the upper division institution as a satisfactory means of providing additional publicly supported education beyond the junior college.

In at least one state, however, creation of upper division institutions was proposed, in the mid-fifties, not as a capstone to existing institutions but as "an arrangement which would encourage the development of community colleges under local auspices" (Fretwell, 1968). By 1956, the statewide system of two-year colleges in New York enrolled about 11,000 students; yet, in certain areas of the state, particularly Long Island, critical shortages of both two- and four-year facilities still existed. Although the state university trustees had already begun planning for a five-year teacher training institution at Oyster Bay (later to become the State University at Stony Brook), "such an institution," the regents concluded, "is of limited scope and will meet only a small part of the needs" (University of the State of New York, 1957b, p. 15).

As early as 1944, during the initial development of plans for a statewide system of community and technical colleges, Commissioner George Stoddard had encouraged the creation of an upper division institution at the New School as a logical and necessary addition to the system (see Chapter Three). Now, in 1956, the regents proposed the creation of three new community colleges for Long Island which, admittedly, "would still leave an unmet need for education beyond two-year opportunities." Therefore, the regents also suggested creation of a "senior college, composed of the junior, senior and first graduate years [which] would serve as a capstone to an integrated educational system (University of the State of New York, 1957b, pp. 15, 16). According to E. K. Fretwell, Jr. (1968), then assistant commissioner and coauthor of the regents' statement, "we knew that we needed at least two more community colleges [on Long Island] and one way to make this thing work was to create a draw-through effect for those people who would start in the community colleges and end up at a baccalaureate program."

Despite the regents' statement, the state university trustees proceeded with their plans for creation of the five-year programs on Long Island. Accordingly, in July 1957, the regents reaffirmed their initial recommendations, developing an eight-point rationale for the creation of "the Community College-Senior College Plan" both on Long Island and in other locations throughout the state. Recognizing the existence of the community colleges—and restating their desirability from an educational viewpoint—the regents stated that "the senior college plan takes account of the merits, increased expansion and importance of community colleges in the structure and development of American higher education." Furthermore, such a system would allow for the development of a rational, decentralized system of community colleges, while "it encourages centralization of upper division learning areas . . . for which expensive laboratory equipment and other facilities are essential." Finally, the regents stated, "the community college-senior college arrangement is already being utilized successfully, particularly in Michigan and California. The University of Michigan, for example, operates a comparable upper division college in Flint taking graduates from the local junior college, and there is a similar proposition pending for Dearborn" (University of the State of New York, 1957a, pp. 9–11).

The trustees, however, were not convinced. Reaffirming

their decision to focus "current efforts on the expansion and development of State University's forty-two established colleges, the creation of additional community colleges . . . and development of a science center on Long Island," the trustees announced their intent "to proceed with implementation of this program as rapidly as possible" (cited by Martorana, 1968). Although no reference was made to the regents' suggestion for development of an upper division institution on Long Island, the unanimous decision to continue with previously approved plans indicated "that the upper-division development for Long Island was a closed issue as the State University Trustees viewed it at that time." Yet, the regents' public support of the upper division concept was unchanged, and their recommendations, although unheeded in the fifties, played a significant role in the development of the first public upper division institution in New York State almost a decade later.

The decision in New York not to establish a new upper division institution in the mid-fifties was based, in part, upon the trustees' conviction that the best course was to proceed with the expansion and development of an existing, comprehensive statewide system of two- and four-year colleges. In Florida, on the other hand, decisions taken in the mid-fifties did lead to the establishment of two upper division institutions, at least in part because Florida had "enjoyed the benefits of a well-managed system of status quo higher education" (Culpepper and Tully, 1967, p. 4) for nearly fifty years. Between 1905—when all public higher education in the state was unified in a state university, college, and normal school under the Buckman Act—and 1954—when a consulting group was engaged by the State Board of Control to initiate "continuing studies basic to the development of a system of higher education in the State which will provide the highest quality programs for the greatest number of people at the lowest possible costs"—the only major change in the system was made in 1946 when both the University of Florida and Florida State College for Women (now Florida State University) were made coeducational.

The consulting group, chaired by A. J. Brumbaugh, former dean of the college at the University of Chicago, and including John E. Ivey, John Dale Russell, and Earl J. McGrath, made its preliminary recommendations to the Board of Control on January 20, 1955. Recognizing that Florida was beginning its planning from an almost nonexistent base of public higher education, the commission recommended immediate establishment of a system of public community colleges, additional state colleges, and a means for coordinating all public and private, two- and four-year higher education within the state. Almost at once, delegations from several metropolitan areas converged upon both the board and the state legislature to begin their bids for the new institutions. The delegation from Hillsboro County (Tampa) introduced legislation to authorize the founding of a new university "in the Tampa Bay area." In order to secure adequate support, the Hillsboro legislators agreed to support a move by the Palm Beach delegation to introduce similar legislation for Palm Beach County; the Palm Beach delegation in turn accepted support from the Pensacola delegation and agreed to an amendment of its legislation to include the words "and Escambia County" (*Laws of Florida,* 1955, pp. 433, 434). Thus, in a single legislative session, even before the Brumbaugh Report had been published, new institutions were authorized for Hillsboro (Tampa), Palm Beach, and Escambia (Pensacola) counties.

The legislation merely authorized establishment; pressure was then brought to bear on the Board of Control to formally implement the legislation. The consultants' report, as finally published in 1956, heartily approved the legislative decision to locate a new institution in Tampa but stated that "the legislation which authorized the establishment of a state university in Palm Beach County is sufficiently restrictive to preclude using it as authority for establishing on the lower East Coast an institution in a location [nearer to Miami] in which it is most needed" (Brumbaugh and Blee, 1956, p. 36). Although never stating that the Palm Beach institution should be abandoned, the report continued by recommending that the Board of Control request "legislation authorizing it, or the Board of Education, to establish an institution in a location in lower Broward or upper Dade County" (p. 36), thirty miles to the south of the proposed Palm Beach locations.

The aggressiveness with which the various communities vied for the new institutions is indicated by the fact that between the initial presentation of the consultants' recommendations and the end of 1956, the Hillsboro delegation made six appearances before the Board of Control to argue its case, while the delegations from Palm Beach and Escambia each appeared four times. Of those counties supported by the consultants' recommendations, the group from Broward was too disorganized, and the group from Dade was "indifferent or openly hostile to any suggestion of locating a public university" to compete with the University of Miami (Whaley, 1970, p. 516); both had slight chance of securing a new institution for their communities.

The Hillsboro delegation, in large part on the strength of the consultants' recommendations, succeeded, on December 18, 1956, in securing a resolution from the Board of Control to establish a new institution in their home county, while the Palm Beach and Escambia delegations continued to jockey for support. On January 7, 1957, the board agreed to accept an abandoned airfield in Boca Raton as a site for the Palm Beach institution if and when such an institution should be established. Following a series of legal delays, the board formally accepted title to the land on August 25, 1968, and on September 18, requested Ivey to prepare a tentative plan. Although the new institution had still to be legally established, the board appeared ready to accede to the legislature and to establish the "East coast" institution in Palm Beach rather than in Broward or Dade.

Proponents of the Escambia institution, however, were not having similar success. Part of this failure was due to initial attempts to secure approval based on the use of Corry Field in Pensacola as a site for the institution; this Navy installation, originally scheduled to be abandoned in June 1958, was eliminated as a possible site on July 19, 1957, following a Navy decision not to build new facilities in southern Alabama. More significant, however, was the attempt to tie creation of a new institution to the conversion of Pensacola Junior College to a four-year program, a move consistently opposed by the State Department of Education and the Board of Control. As early as July 17, 1956, the Pensacola Chamber of Commerce had petitioned the board to convert the junior college to a four-year program; repeated attempts to secure approval, both at the board and in the legislature, were defeated over the next two years. Finally, despite local estimates that a four-year institution would enroll between 1,500 and 2,500 students, the board declared that it "saw no need for a university in the Pensacola area in the foreseeable future" (*Pensacola Journal,* 1957b)" and that it would not approve conversion of the junior college for that purpose.

Thus, despite the legislative authorization secured two years earlier, the Pensacola institution was defeated—at least for the remainder of the fifties. On the other hand, the Boca Raton institution, although not yet formally established, appeared very much alive. On November 1, 1959, Ivey presented his recommendations to the board. In a report later characterized (Williams, 1968) as "both too idealistic and too expensive," Ivey (1959, pp. 2–4) proposed that Florida use the Boca Raton facilities to create "a laboratory for demonstrating approaches to the numbers-quality dilemma in Florida and the nation" and "a high quality potential." "The University at Boca Raton," Ivey concluded, "should be planned from the outset as a graduate institution." Furthermore, the proposed community colleges in the area would "offer the possibility of a new type of cooperation between a university and several junior colleges." Thus, if the board also wished to offer undergraduate education at the new institution, "it would be unnecessary for the University to offer an extensive program of freshman and sophomore work on its campus."

Although the Ivey Report made passing reference to undergraduate instruction, its basic emphasis was on graduate education to serve the intellectual, industrial, and scientific needs of the area. This seeming failure to provide for a baccalaureate-granting institution in southeast Florida, Ivey's return to New York, and some basic misgivings on the part of several members of the Board of Control led the board to request that Brumbaugh return to Florida to "complete" the work which Ivey had started. Thus, in 1959, four years after the initial authorization of a Palm Beach institution and a full year after the selection of a site, a new study was begun. Here, as at Pensacola, the first steps had been taken toward creation of a new institution which, during the following decade, would become an upper division and graduate level university.

The decisions involving the two Florida institutions and the creation of Flint College in Michigan required several years to reach because of political and financial complications which were compounded, in each case, by a lack of distinct resolve on the part of the establishing body that a new institution was truly needed or justified. The decisions involving the final upper division institution established during the fifties—Dearborn College—were reached, on the other hand, within fifteen months after negotiations were begun between the University of Michigan and the Ford Motor Company. The rapidity with which the necessary steps were taken was a reflection of both the political power of the Ford Motor Company and a genuine merging of interests on the part of the two groups participating in the decision.

The Dearborn institution, to which the July 1957 New York State regents' report made reference, had its beginnings in a series of developments within both the Ford Motor Company and the State of Michigan dating back to the early twentieth century. At that time, the Ford Company had begun a number of industrial education programs for its employees, including a trade school and an industrial engineering school which offered college-level engineering training for professional employees. In 1947, as part of a general reorganization instituted by the new president, Henry Ford II, the company decided to eliminate these "captive teaching staffs" and to draw upon existing educational institutions for classroom instruction, in part because of the increasing difficulty of securing high-quality scholars for an in-house educational program. The trade school was liquidated in 1952, and its assets, totaling approximately $1.5 million, were turned over to the Dearborn Board of Education, which used the funds to build and equip an industrial education facility for the local junior college, soon renamed the Henry Ford Junior College. By 1956, the last of the full-time industrial classroom programs of the company ended.[1]

Concurrently, the company began a series of studies to determine its on-going manpower needs and to identify resources to meet them. An extensive study, initiated in 1954 and completed in

[1] Background discussion concerning Ford Motor Company is based on Saltzman, 1968.

February 1955, indicated that the company would require approximately 1,150 new college graduates each year, about two-thirds of whom would ultimately serve in managerial and engineering positions in the manufacturing and assembly plants. Yet, past experience had shown engineering graduates reluctant to enter manufacturing engineering (as opposed to product engineering), and business graduates were loath to enter plant management. A decision was reached, during the summer of 1955, to explore possible means of encouraging local community college graduates—seen as a new pool from which to recruit personnel—to enter the production area and then to acquire engineering or management credentials or both.

In August of that same year, Archie A. Pearson, manager of the company corporate-level training department, conceived the idea of developing a Ford facility to provide the required education for community college graduates and of inviting nearby public and private institutions of higher education to offer junior and senior level courses which might lead to engineering or business degrees. Following company approval of the idea, Pearson contacted R. H. Scott, a professor of management at Wayne University and a personal friend, to explore the concept; Scott recommended working through one institution, such as the University of Michigan, rather than attempting to deal with a number of institutions and boards of control. Taking this suggestion, Pearson next approached another friend, James Lewis, vice president of student affairs at the University of Michigan, and, through Lewis' efforts, met with Niehuss, executive vice president of the university, on August 31, 1955.

The University of Michigan was in an excellent position to be receptive to Pearson's ideas. Just seven months earlier, under Niehuss' direction, the negotiations leading to university approval of an upper division unit in Flint had been secured, setting a precedent for the location of other units outside Ann Arbor. One reason for the willingness of the university to establish additional units, as seen by the Ford representatives, was the on-going campaign to create new state universities from former teachers' colleges and to create a state institution at Wayne University, then a Detroit municipal institution. Each newly created state university meant additional competition for state funds, and legislative loyalty was more often tied to local institutions than to the University of Michigan, which served a truly international clientele. Thus, the University of Michigan, as well as Michigan State University, was eager to establish a base of operations in several locations, especially Detroit, in order to secure some portion of the legislative support of that locality. Although this hypothesis has never been directly stated by a representative of the University of Michigan, the Saltzman document, prepared at the request of the author, which gives many of the internal happenings at Ford, indicated that this was a reason for the willingness of the university to move into Detroit. That document received clearance from officials of the university before Saltzman forwarded it to the author.

Initial conversations between Lewis and Niehuss, from the university, and Pearson and C. H. Anderson, director of personnel, from Ford, concerned the Ford proposal for a cooperative education center in Dearborn. Almost immediately, the university suggested development of a separate branch, similar to that in Flint, which would be independent of Ford and open to all students on an equal basis but would offer programs of study which both Ford and the university deemed desirable. Neither Ford nor the university ever seriously considered development of a lower division; Ford needs were centered at the upper division and graduate level, and the university had no desire to duplicate either its own Ann Arbor offerings or those of the local community college (Niehuss, 1968). On January 16, 1956, the Administration Committee at Ford heard a report of the preliminary discussions and appointed a formal negotiating committee, chaired by Vice President John S. Bugas and including Pearson, Anderson, and Arthur W. Saltzman of Pearson's department. The Administration Committee also tentatively agreed to provide a cash grant and building site for the proposed institution and requested that the university be asked to consider graduate education and an extensive cooperative education program with Ford in its planning (Ford Motor Company, 1956).

Concurrently, the university appointed a committee, chaired by Niehuss and including Deans Lewis and Dorr, dean for statewide education, to meet with Ford. On February 17, the two committees, joined by Hatcher, met to formalize agreements to that point. The university agreed to include graduate and cooperative educational programs, and the two committees agreed to meet over the next few months to develop specific curricular proposals. At the following meeting, on March 2, the committees agreed—at the insistence of the university—that the new facility should offer baccalaureate-level liberal arts programs as well; it was also decided to organize the calendar on a quarter system to facilitate the cooperative programs and to notify the Dearborn Community College (not yet renamed) of the negotiations which were in progress. Dorr notified the community college president the following week, and the Dearborn Board of Education received official notification at its April meeting.

Negotiations proceeded smoothly during April. Deans Brown (engineering) and Taggart (business) began both academic and space requirement plans, aiming toward deadlines of May 1 and June 1, respectively. Planning goals were set for a resident student body, in engineering and business, of 500 undergraduates and 250 graduate students, of whom approximately 60 per cent would be assigned to the Ford Motor Company for their cooperative experience; since, under the cooperative plan, one-half of all registered students would be working off campus, these projections meant a total student body of 1,000 undergraduates and 500 graduate students. In addition, the plan provided for 1,000 undergraduate liberal arts students, not engaged in a cooperative program, bringing the total planned enrollment to approximately 2,500 students (University of Michigan, 1956a).

The university planning document was ready for presentation to the Ford representatives by late July. Based on the projected enrollments two sets of estimates, the recommended and the minimum, were developed in terms of square feet and dollars. After considerable study of the university figures, Ford agreed to offer a grant of $6.5 million (about halfway between the two university figures), exclusive of land, for the development of the Dearborn center. On September 14, 1956, Ford and the university reached agreement on the procedures for requesting the gifts; rather than ask the company directly for money, the university was to request money from the Ford Fund (the charitable fund of the company) and land from the Ford Foundation, which held title to the property under consideration (University of Michigan, 1956b). Following Bugas' successful clearance of these arrangements with top fund and foundation officials, Pearson and Saltzman reported to Niehuss on October 4 that the fund "will welcome a request from the University for $6,500,000" but that the company had decided to offer Fair Lane, the Ford family estate, rather than the land held in title by the foundation (Saltzman, 1968).

By November 2, 1956, all was in readiness for formal application to the Ford Fund and the Ford Motor Company. Request documents and letters had been jointly reviewed and cleared by the Ford legal department, and a timetable for submission (November 5) and review (November 6 and 7) had been established (University of Michigan, 1956c). In accordance with these plans, Hatcher sent separate letters to the fund and to the company, outlining the desire of the university "to extend our program to a select area outside of Ann Arbor" as a means "of meeting the need for more college-trained graduates in specialty fields." After briefly describing the program to be offered, Hatcher (1956) stated that "the University invites the Ford Motor Company [or Ford Fund] to participate in the development of this proposed educational center" through a gift of the Fair Lane properties plus 210 acres, in one case, and through a donation of $6.5 million, in the other.

In an accompanying document, the university (1956d) tied its Dearborn requests to a larger, statewide, "planned program of expansion in keeping with its history and responsibility to the State." The components of the program as stated in this document were similar to suggestions originally made by Gorman in late 1954 as a means of breaking the deadlock in the university-Flint negotiations: "extension of the University's facilities to other communities in the State where clear needs exist and where such communities are prepared to assist the State by contributing toward the cost of new facilities" and willingness to establish upper division programs where "the operation of the college will be in close cooperation with the existing junior college."

Official announcement of the offer was made at the Fair Lane estate in a joint news conference held December 17, 1956, by

Hatcher and Ford. On January 6, 1957, a joint meeting of the Michigan house and senate voted unanimously "that this body urges The Regents of the University of Michigan to accept this generous gift" (Merrill, 1957). The formal offer, conveyed in writing to Hatcher on January 24, 1957, was "gratefully accepted" by the regents at their regular meeting on February 16, 1957. Thirty months later, in the fall of 1959, the University of Michigan— Dearborn Center opened with thirty-four students.

Six

Rise of the Pragmatists

By 1960, four upper division institutions were in operation. Two, Concordia Senior College and the New School College, were private institutions serving narrowly defined populations; each resulted from decisions taken during the 1940's, before the full effects of the development of public junior colleges and the postwar needs of the national economy had been felt. The other two institutions, branches of the University of Michigan developed during the 1950's in Flint and Dearborn, were public colleges serving the general population of Michigan; although Flint College was designed to meet an anticipated increase in student demand and the Dearborn campus was designed to fill the need of industry for a specific type of college graduate, each institution reflected both the existence of a growing system of junior colleges in the state and the increased demand for baccalaureate-educated citizens.

The growth of public junior colleges in Michigan was typical of the growth of similar institutions throughout most sections of the United States during the 1950's and 1960's. In Florida, the system of public junior colleges had grown from five institutions enrolling approximately 1,000 students in 1955 to twenty-nine institutions enrolling over 40,000 students by 1962. In New York City—as in New York State—public junior, or community, colleges also experienced rapid growth; in 1956, two public community colleges in the city enrolled fewer than 2,500 students; by 1961, five institutions served over 9,000 students. By 1965, the total enrollment in both Florida and New York City again doubled, while other areas, such as Pennsylvania, began new systems of public junior, or community, colleges.

Moreover, the existing junior colleges broadened their offerings to include more vocational or technological courses to meet the growing needs of industry and government for trained manpower below the baccalaureate level. Concurrently, the demand for baccalaureate education grew, partially because of the postwar baby boom, which reached its peak for colleges during the sixties, partially because increasing percentages of the general population were continuing their education beyond high school or junior college, and partially because of the influence of the junior colleges themselves. In many states, including Florida and New York, the system of public junior colleges brought the first two years of college to within commuting distance and financial reach of many students who could not afford four years of college away from home. These same students, who otherwise might not have begun their college education, then added to the demand for baccalaureate-level offerings.

As more junior college students completed the associate degree and entered four-year institutions, the four-year institutions themselves faced new problems. In many instances, junior year classes—swelled by junior college transfers—exceeded freshman year classes in total enrollment, despite normal attrition rates following each year of collegiate study. The problem was magnified for public institutions, whose low tuition (and, in some areas, legal commitment to accept junior college graduates) made them more desirable than private schools, particularly for those students who had attended a junior college rather than a four-year college for economic reasons. The concept of educational opportunity for all, despite its social benefits, created severe problems for some institutions or systems of public higher education.

In no case was the existence of many community college graduates the only reason for creation of an upper division college, although the presence of a sizable pool of graduates was a prerequisite for an upper division institution. In Flint and Dearborn, the existence of the junior colleges both reinforced the demand for increased baccalaureate offerings and obviated the need to re-create the freshman and sophomore years in a new four-year institution. Moreover, four-year colleges would not provide sufficient additional space at the junior year once their own sophomores had been accommodated. Increasingly throughout the 1960's, communities or systems of education determined a need for increased baccalaureate offerings (based, to some extent but never exclusively, upon growing numbers of community college graduates); the result of this perceived need often was an upper division institution.

Thus, in the mid-1950's, the Brumbaugh Commission in Florida recommended establishment of additional baccalaureate-level institutions along with a comprehensive system of public junior colleges (see Chapter Five). In 1959, the report of John E. Ivey (pp. 3–4) on implementing the Brumbaugh recommendations in southeast Florida suggested creation of "a quality institution" with "a new type of cooperation between a university and several junior colleges" which would make it "unnecessary for the University to offer an extensive program of freshman and sophomore work on its campus." Ivey's report was accepted by the Florida Board of Control in November 1959, "subject to further refinements and revisions"; in May 1960, A. J. Brumbaugh was appointed by the board "to evaluate and to refine the tentative plans provided to the Board by Dr. John E. Ivey, Jr." (cited by Brumbaugh, 1961, p. 1).

Ivey's report emphasized the development of graduate programs and of a series of institutes which would make use of new educational technology (such as television) and would provide research and development services for the populous southeast coast. Yet, Ivey's concept of undergraduate education was unclear, despite the suggestion (pp. 10–13) of "cooperation" with junior colleges and a broad description of a "General College . . . responsible for general education throughout the student's baccalaureate program." The general college would include lower and upper division work and would be coordinated with the work of the institutes, spanning both the undergraduate and graduate years.

On December 10, 1960, Brumbaugh made his first report to the board. "The University," he stated, "will look to the community junior colleges of the State, and especially those in the southeastern coastal area, to provide the basic education of the freshman and sophomore years." While maintaining the same stress on academic excellence and service to the community which had characterized the Ivey Report, Brumbaugh's report was much more specific as to how the baccalaureate education which the region required would be provided. "In effect," Brumbaugh (1961, p. 4) wrote in the published draft, "the lower division program of the university will be decentralized and allocated to the junior colleges, while the upper level, the usual junior and senior years, will be concentrated on the university campus."

Ivey's basic concept of a reduced freshman and sophomore program was now a plan for an institution without any freshman or sophomore years, an upper division institution. Yet, this basic decision may have been made even before Brumbaugh was retained to conduct his study. As early as January 4, 1960, Executive Director (later Chancellor) J. Broward Culpepper circulated a paper entitled "Next Steps for Creating the State University at Boca Raton," which proposed creating the university "along the unique lines envisioned in the plan." Since Ivey's was the only published plan at that time, "the plan" must have been either that of Ivey or one suggested by another member of the staff before Brumbaugh's arrival. Similarly, Culpepper's "Summary of Plans for a State University at Boca Raton"—although undated—may be placed between completion of the Ivey Report and the beginning of the Brumbaugh study from its reference to "the main ideas contained in the *Tentative Plan for a State University at Boca Raton*" (the Ivey Report) and its failure to mention the establishment of a new planning body. Culpepper's summary states that "the University will place primary emphasis on an upper division program on the assumption that satisfactory cooperative arrangements can be made with the community junior colleges to provide high quality basic education."

Culpepper has written (1969) that "the idea of developing a new institution where the emphasis is upon upper level undergraduate and graduate work was reviewed well before the Brumbaugh report of 1961, . . . which was supposed to be a follow-up on the Ivey report to crystalize in more detailed fashion the steps which might be followed for developing the new institution." Brumbaugh himself has written (1968) that "the concept of an upper division institution to be established at Boca Raton, Florida, emerged from consideration of several possibilities by the Planning Commission of which I was director," including Ivey's general college, Culpepper's "primary emphasis on an upper division program," and the ultimate plan for a "decentralized" lower division relegated to the local community colleges. Furthermore, Brumbaugh "quite naturally was committed to the lower-division and upper-division model" (1968) from his experience in establishing the college program at the University of Chicago in the 1930's.

According to Kenneth R. Williams (1968)—then president of Dade County Junior College (later Miami-Dade Junior College) and of the Florida Association of Public Junior Colleges, one of the "resource persons" utilized in Brumbaugh's study, and later to become the first president of the institution—Brumbaugh's recommendations were based on three major considerations: a desire for a research oriented and scholarly university unhampered by the freshman and sophomore years of general education (drawn from the Ivey Report), a hesitancy to duplicate the offerings of existing junior college programs, and a wish to create an innovative structure for higher education. To these considerations Culpepper (1969) has added "the emphasis on economy in government" under the new governor, Farris Bryant. Brumbaugh, however, was not as concerned with the innovative aspects of the institution as Williams has assumed; "the institution was created," according to Brumbaugh, "as a response to local pragmatic needs as opposed to educational theories based on known or assumed models" (1968).

Plans for an upper division institution, regardless of their educational foundation, had a strong basis in realistic political considerations. Many legislators felt that the existing programs at Tallahassee (Florida State University) and Gainesville (University of Florida) were in desperate need of support and that new institutions should not be created until these had been strengthened. Brumbaugh's proposals, by assuring the seven counties of southeastern Florida that their new or proposed community colleges would not be threatened, gathered vastly needed legislative support for the proposed institution at Boca Raton. In addition, Brumbaugh's proposals implied warm praise for the community colleges; the new institution not only would be designed as a continuation rather than a competition for these colleges but also would recognize their merit by building a quality program on top of their preparation.

The Board of Control formally adopted Brumbaugh's report on July 15, 1961, and in the 1961 legislative session, money was appropriated for staffing the newly named Florida Atlantic University in Boca Raton. Williams was appointed president on May 11, 1962, and he began to assemble a staff and develop detailed plans for his "unique institution, unlike any other in the nation" (n.d., p. 3). If any of the existing upper division institutions had been used as models by Brumbaugh or Culpepper, who later (1969) wrote that "we were not influenced by other institutions," Williams was not aware of them. As stated in the second catalogue (1965a, p. 17), "the establishment of Florida Atlantic University is the culmination of years of dedicated effort on the part of civic leaders, government officials and educators to bring a state institution of higher learning to the populous lower east coast of Florida. . . . It is the first in the nation to forego freshman and sophomore classes."

The original Brumbaugh Report, published in 1956, recognized that the location authorized by the legislature in Palm Beach County was sufficiently far removed from Miami to warrant consideration of an additional institution in that metropolitan area. Yet, Brumbaugh's 1961 report, which became the basic planning document for the Boca Raton institution, made no apparent distinction between the need for an institution serving "the lower east coast" from Boca Raton and for one serving from Broward or Dade to the south. Williams has implied (1968) that both Ivey and Brumbaugh assumed that the location of the new institution might still be other than at Boca Raton, even after the board had taken title to the land in August 1958. Nonetheless, despite some local feelings in Boca Raton that the proposed site might better be used as an industrial park, the board decided to accept the available site and to retain the possibility of creating another institution farther south at a later date.

In retrospect, it seems apparent that the location of this institution should have been closer to the metropolitan Miami area. Although earlier statements concerning Florida Atlantic saw "the opportunity [to extend] higher education to the increasing numbers of Florida's college age youth, particularly those in the populous lower east coast of the State," more recent documents (State Board of Regents of Florida, 1968, p. 2) concluded that "although the establishing of Florida Atlantic University in south Palm Beach County in 1962 made a public degree-granting institution generally available to young people in the lower east coast of Florida, the need for a similar institution more central to metropolitan Dade remains undiminished." Thus, a new upper division institution, Florida International University, will begin operation in the Miami area in 1972.

Brumbaugh's 1961 report did make a number of correct assumptions with respect to the direction of higher education in Florida, especially with regard to the need, both educationally and politically, to protect the growing system of public junior colleges. All new institutions offering a baccalaureate within the Florida public system, with the exception of Florida Technological University in Orlando, have been or are being planned as upper division institutions. These new institutions include Florida International (Dade) and the University of North Florida (Duval), both scheduled to begin operation in 1972. The 1964 master plan, which also recommended establishment of a new public institution in Dade County, drew upon Brumbaugh's analysis of community college-senior college relations to propose a series of state urban colleges, each to be an upper division institution drawing upon local community colleges and serving a heavily populated area. The recommendation was followed, although political pressure from urban areas following reapportionment in 1963 forced creation of new "universities" rather than "colleges" beginning at the junior year.

By 1963, "the public policy structure (the Board of Control, its chief executive officer, Dr. Broward Culpepper, certain legislators, and the Governor, and so forth) had committed itself to the model provided by the Brumbaugh Commission Report for Florida Atlantic University" (Stallworth, 1968). This commitment, although not so obviously stated at the time, was a factor in and was reinforced by the decisions regarding the establishment of the new institution in Pensacola. The campaign to develop the Pensacola institution, first authorized in 1955 and promoted unsuccessfully by various groups from Pensacola and Escambia County (see Chapter Five) through the remainder of the fifties, was given new life on March 22, 1961, when Bryant stated that Pensacola Junior College should be converted to a four-year institution (*Pensacola News,* 1961a). The following day, the Pensacola Chamber of Commerce suggested that the Board of Control focus its energies on creating a four-year program in Pensacola rather than continuing with development of the new institution in Boca Raton (*Florida Times Union,* 1961).

Although the Board of Control had already stated, on March 21, 1958, that it would not support conversion of Pensacola Junior College to a four-year institution, it met with the Pensacola delegation on April 21, 1961, and announced that it "would give serious consideration to the matter." There is no record of pressures brought to bear upon the board; yet, the demand for an institution in Pensacola was receiving active political support in early 1961, and the president of the junior college, Henry Ashmore, had gone on record as preferring conversion of his institution to creation of a new college, primarily for financial reasons. Bryant, whose statement of support for conversion signaled the start of the new campaign in March, included $100,000 "planning money for a four-year college in Pensacola" (*Pensacola Journal,* 1961b) in his 1961 budget request on April 5 and called for a study of the need of the west Florida area for a four-year institution.

Despite the recognition in the *Pensacola News* of April 6, 1961, that "the Board of Control, in former years, has opposed any move to expand a junior college into a four-year degree-granting institution," proponents of the conversion of Pensacola Junior College introduced legislation in both houses of the state legislature the following week to create West Florida State College as an institution which would combine the services of a two- and four-year institution. The day before the Board of Control agreed to study the matter further, the conversion legislation cleared its first major hurdle and was reported out of the House Committee on Higher Education; five days later, the Senate Education Committee also approved the measure. Yet, on May 11, 1961, the board again reversed its position, stating its support of an appropriation for planning but restating its opposition to the conversion of any two-year institutions. Despite its early legislative successes, the appropriations legislation (*Laws of Florida,* 1961, p. 780) for the Pensacola college was finally passed in June without reference to conversion of the junior college.

The variety of the responses which the conversion legislation received can be explained in part by the make-up of the house and senate and their various committees. Proponents of the conversion—primarily among delegates from Escambia County—had significantly more strength in the committees than in the legislature as a whole. Moreover, the initial authorizing legislation passed in 1955 had been based upon a series of agreements with Palm Beach and Hillsboro counties which had implied a definite order for the establishment of the new institutions: Hillsboro, Palm Beach, and then Escambia; some legislators saw the Escambia delegation actions as an attempt to break this agreement and to secure an institution before Palm Beach County did. Finally, some legislators who had encountered difficulty in securing local support for newly created junior colleges in their areas did not want any legislation which might imply that junior colleges were not completely satisfactory in themselves.

Following appropriation of $100,000 for a study in Pensacola, the next move was up to the Board of Control. On February 16, 1962, the board appointed Professor John Guy Fowlkes of the

University of Wisconsin to conduct a study of the educational needs in the Pensacola area, and on March 8 and 9, Fowlkes and Culpepper visited Pensacola with John C. Pace, a member of the Board of Control from that city. By March 16, Fowlkes reported to the board that the outline and the instruments for the study had been completed and that he hoped to have a final report ready by mid-summer. Yet, disagreements over the purpose of Fowlkes' study appear to have remained, for the board felt the necessity to state (*Pensacola Journal,* 1962) on May 11 that "the 1961 Session of the Legislature appropriated $100,000 to the Board of Control for the purpose of planning for a four-year college at Pensacola. We have interpreted the word 'planning' to mean a study and determination of needs in the Pensacola area and the planning of such institution as the study might indicate as needed in the area." To which Pace replied that the last thing Pensacola needed was another study of need. "Bring it out, Culpepper," Pace said, "and show us whether it is a boy or a girl."

Pace need not have worried about the results of the study. The Fowlkes Report (1962a), made public at an open meeting of the Board of Control at the San Carlos Hotel in Pensacola on July 21, 1962, was unconditional in its recommendations for the establishment of a four-year college for Pensacola. In view of subsequent events, it is worth citing the entire relevant paragraph from Fowlkes' draft of July 21, 1962 (p. 51): "If the primary focus of the Pensacola Junior College is study leading to a collegiate degree, it would seem that a 4-year institution would assume practically all the functions of the Pensacola Junior College. It must not be inferred, however, that this would necessarily be the case, for there are ample illustrations where the comprehensive community college with functions and clientele significantly different from that interested in a degree-granting institution of higher learning could and should prevail with a 4-year institution in or nearby the community junior college." Fowlkes' conclusion, reported the following day in all Pensacola papers, was that "the data previously presented build a forceful case for the establishment of a four-year institution within the Pensacola area not later than 1970" (p. 70).

Supporters of a four-year college were pleased, although the

Fowlkes Report had not recommended conversion of the junior college as some had hoped. Throughout the next several months, advocates of conversion—including Ashmore, the Pensacola City Council, the Escambia County Commission, and the Citizen's Committee for a Four-Year College for Pensacola—made numerous public statements in favor of conversion, hoping that the board might act on Fowlkes' recommendation to establish a four-year college but ignore his conclusion that a two- and a four-year college could successfully operate within the same community. Yet, despite the public debate over the way a four-year college should be created, by late October Culpepper and his staff had already rejected both proposals in favor of a third option, creation of an upper division institution.

According to the *Pensacola News-Journal* (1957), the State Board of Control "approved a four-year college for Pensacola." Yet, a close reading of the minutes of the board shows that it did not do so. Following Culpepper's introduction of Fowlkes, Fowlkes "discussed at length and in great detail the contents of the study to establish a four-year college in Pensacola, Florida." After questions from citizens who attended the meeting and "after considerable discussion by members of the Board, Dr. Culpepper, Dr. Fowlkes, and others, Mr. Pace moved that the following actions recommended by Dr. Culpepper be taken by the Board concerning the establishment of a *degree-granting* institution in the Pensacola area: that the Board of Control recommend to the 1963 Session of the Legislature the establishment of a *degree-granting* institution in the Pensacola area" (State Board of Control of Florida, 1961–1964, pp. 290–292, italics mine).

According to Phillip F. Ashler (1968)—former administrator at Pensacola Junior College, member of the legislature, and now vice chancellor of the state university system in Florida—the wording of the original Fowlkes Report, which proposed a four-year institution, was probably a semantic error made before the implications of such a statement were apparent. Furthermore, according to Culpepper (1969), "during that time of conflict [after July 21, 1962] I took the position that the nature and type of the new institution should be based upon a plan of organization which would meet most effectively the needs of the state. . . . I do not have any recollection of changes being made in the Fowlkes report."

Yet, on October 30, 1962, Culpepper's assistant, Herbert Stallworth, wrote to Fowlkes to report completion of the typing of the final draft of Fowlkes's study. "Of the corrections indicated on the manuscript, most are typographical errors," Stallworth wrote (1962b). "Also, when reference is made to the proposed institution in the Pensacola area, the institution is designated as a 'degree-granting' rather than a 'four-year' institution." The final report (Fowlkes, 1962b), as typed and produced in Tallahassee, included at least one other significant change from the original Fowlkes draft; the paragraph which discussed the relationship of the community college to the four-year institution now read (p. 64, italics mine): "If the primary focus of the Pensacola Junior College is study leading to a collegiate degree, it would seem that a *degree-granting* institution would assume practically all of the functions of the Pensacola Junior College. It must not be inferred, however, that this would necessarily be the case. *First, such a degree-granting institution would not necessarily be a four-year institution.* Second, even assuming a four-year degree-granting institution, there are ample illustrations where the comprehensive community college with functions and clientele significantly different from those found in degree-granting institutions continue to render valuable service in a community where there is also a four-year degree-granting institution."

Regardless of the reasons for such a change, it appears that a decision was made to modify the wording of the Fowlkes study after the July meeting at which the report was originally presented. Fowlkes has stated (1969) that he was not consulted about any changes in wording and that his considered opinion was that a four-year institution—rather than either a converted junior college or an upper division institution—could be justified and should be established in Pensacola. The modifications in the text of the Fowlkes Report did not eliminate the possibility of a four-year institution; they merely extended the options available to the board in terms of organizational patterns. Moreover, it was important, because of the political and emotional climate in Pensacola, that the final recommendation from the board be supported by Fowlkes's report to avoid putting the board itself in a difficult position. Even though Fowlkes had never considered an upper division institution, Culpepper (1964, p. 1) wrote in his report to the board the following year that "on the basis of an educational study directed by John Guy Fowlkes of the University of Wisconsin, the Board of Control and the State Board of Education decided to establish an upper-level institution (juniors and seniors) in the Pensacola area."

Regardless of the private considerations which followed Fowlkes's presentation in July, two public questions remained: Should a new institution be established in Pensacola to provide baccalaureate-level education, and if so, what form should it take? The public decision for the first question had already been announced in the affirmative; privately, it appears that the decision to the second question was made in the months between the public board meeting and the publication of Fowlkes's study in October. Yet, a number of events occurred before, on February 8, 1963, the board announced its public decision on the form of the institution.

As stated above, public pressure for conversion of the junior college continued even after the July board meeting at which Fowlkes had justified coexistence of a two- and four-year institution in the same community. On October 29, 1962, Stallworth (1962a) prepared a detailed rebuttal for Culpepper of an anonymous paper dated September 1962 and entitled "The Case for Conversion of the Pensacola Junior College." This rebuttal, "made with vast enthusiasm and high passion" (Stallworth, 1968), did not advocate any alternate form of organization, although it did present positive arguments for both a four-year institution and an upper division institution as alternatives to the proposed conversion of the junior college. Concurrently, informal discussions among the staff members of the Board of Control and the State Junior College Advisory Board were being held to consider alternatives to conversion of the junior college.

On November 15, 1962, the State Junior College Advisory Board formally constituted a committee, including Executive Secretary James L. Wattenbarger, "to work with a similar committee from the Board of Control to develop a statement regarding Pensacola Junior College" (1962). The first draft of that document, dated January 8, 1963, presented a detailed rebuttal of the arguments for conversion of the junior college and recommended that "the Board of Control request of the 1963 Session of the Legislature the establishment of an upper level degree-granting institution in the Pensacola area" (State Board of Control of Florida, 1963, p. 6). The Junior College Advisory Board considered the report at its meeting on January 17, and passed it unanimously with the understanding that "if when the Board of Control considered the report, minor changes in wording were desirable, . . . Mr. Wattenbarger and Mr. Van Priest were authorized to make such changes for the Board" (1963).

Final approval of the document—with less emphasis on the rebuttal and more emphasis on the positive service which the Pensacola Junior College would perform in cooperation with an upper division institution—was voted unanimously at the meeting of the Board of Control on February 8, 1963 (1961–1964). Yet, as late as January 23, Stallworth (1963) had written to Culpepper reaffirming his support for an independent four-year institution as suggested by Fowlkes for "educational reasons" but recognizing that "the choice on the basis of elements present in the real situation in which we find ourselves is the two-year institution" which, nonetheless, could add freshman and sophomore classes "when it is auspicious to do so should such a move come to be considered to make good sense."

The decision to establish an upper division institution in Pensacola, formally made on February 8, 1963, was the result of a number of factors. Perhaps most basic was the determination by Fowlkes in 1962 that a four-year program could be justified in Pensacola, even though this view was diametrically opposed to the decision of the board in late 1958. Although never stated, one reason for support of Fowlkes's position might have been the realization that some alternative was needed to plans to convert the junior college; the board had consistently rejected all conversion attempts, for educational reasons, because it might lead to wholesale conversion of other institutions and because at least from the statements of the board, the need for a four-year program had not been demonstrated. Board action to create a new institution based on the earlier community demands would be difficult to defend against those supporting conversion; the logical answer was for the board to develop its own independent statement of need, not tied to proposals for conversion, from which it could then determine the most satisfactory response.

Once the board had admitted need, several forms of organization were available. Despite continuous pressure to convert the junior college, the board had never (with the one exception on April 21, 1961, discussed above) so much as agreed to seriously consider such a proposal. The two remaining alternatives—creation of an independent four-year institution and creation of an upper division institution—were both considered, and despite the fact that educational considerations may have lent support to the complete four-year institution, "elements present in the real situation" led to the ultimate decision to create a two-year institution which would extend the local junior college.

Few educational reasons were ever presented to justify this decision, although Wattenbarger later stated that "the tremendous growth of the two-year college has enabled the four-year institution to cut down on its freshman enrollment . . . and is leading to the creation of four-year senior institutions which will not offer the first two years of undergraduate study at all" (cited by "Florida Master Plans for Record College Enrollment," 1965, p. 11). Admittedly, the board already had a model on which to base its new plans: Florida Atlantic University had already been approved and had been justified on the basis of two detailed planning reports. Yet, the decision of Florida Atlantic had itself developed "as a response to local pragmatic needs as opposed to educational theories based on known or assumed models" (Brumbaugh, 1968).

According to Ashler (1968), then a member of the House Committee on Higher Education, the decision of the board was based on Culpepper's opposition to conversion of any junior colleges and on the strength of the Escambia County delegation in the legislature; Ashler felt that the Escambia delegation (of which he was a member) could have secured approval for some type of institution during the 1963 legislative session and that the decision to establish a second upper division before an appropriate trial period at Florida Atlantic (which would not open until 1964) was primarily a result of pressure from the Escambia County delegation within the Florida legislature. According to Ashler, board opposition to the new institution—or at least to its opening before the 1970 date suggested by Fowlkes—was further demonstrated by the fact that the board recommended funding of the university as the fifty-first priority in its 1963 budgetary request, even following a request by Governor Haydon Burns that this priority be revised. Culpepper (1969), however, has stated that a decision to wait until 1970 would have increased the costs involved in developing a new institution; moreover, "the political and community pressures were such that we could not adhere to this recommendation [for a 1970 opening]."

Regardless of the Fowlkes recommendation, the 1963 legislature did appropriate $2.1 million for the "establishment of the West Florida University, a degree-granting institution in Escambia County . . . to begin operations at the junior class level of the undergraduate program not later than September, 1967" (*Laws of Florida*, 1963, p. 750). Following this appropriation, the board also moved swiftly. By September 12, 1963, it had selected a permanent site and within the following year had chosen a president. The Escambia County Commission, in slightly over a year, completed both the bond validation suit and the condemnation proceedings necessary for acquisition of the land for the main campus. Three years later, in September 1967, the University of West Florida opened with 1,318 students.

This initial enrollment gave it the largest first-year class of any of the existing upper division institutions; in fact, with the exception of Concordia College—which was developed with a maximum capacity of 450 students—and the New School College—which had never set enrollment goals since it did not create any new courses or facilities for its baccalaureate programs—the University of West Florida was the first upper division institution to exceed its planning estimates in its first-year class. Florida Atlantic University, which had expected approximately 1,000 students, had enrolled 867 during its first semester, while both Flint College (1,000 by 1959) and Dearborn College (2,500 at full capacity) had begun their operations with a fraction of their projected number of students.

Flint College, which had begun in 1956 with an enrollment of 167 students (see Chapter Five), had resulted from long and often confused negotiations between the University of Michigan—which originally supported a four-year college in Flint—and the Flint community, which wanted a four-year program available in Flint. The enrollment jumped to 356 in its second year, although a large percentage of this increase was due to the inclusion of both a junior and a senior class on campus for the first time. Over the next several years, enrollment continued to climb, although the rate of increase—from 399 in 1958 and 450 in 1959 to only 525 by 1962—was not at all what had been expected. Speaking in late 1962 at a public hearing on the future of Delta College—a community college which was being considered for conversion to a four-year institution—Roger Heyns, vice president for academic affairs at the University of Michigan, admitted that he was "frankly puzzled" by the apparent reluctance of junior college students to pursue their education at either the Flint or the Dearborn campuses of the university (cited by *Flint Journal*, 1962b).

During its early years of operation, Flint College enjoyed good working relations with Flint Junior College, from which it drew over half its student body. The original agreements between the two institutions were expanded and modified on several occasions, including a renegotiation of the basic contract for buildings and maintenance in early 1959 and the decision in February 1961 —based upon an offer of additional facilities from the Mott Foundation—to cooperate in the development of a joint library facility. Yet, despite the lack of friction between the two institutions, minor administrative difficulties arose. In addition, representatives of both the community and the university were concerned about the failure of Flint College to achieve the enrollment anticipated in the mid-fifties.

The initial suggestion in 1962 to reconsider the status of Flint College and the possibility of its becoming a four-year unit came from representatives of the Flint community, according to

Marvin Niehuss (1968) (executive vice president and dean of faculty at the university), David French (1968) (dean of Flint College since its inception), and Lawrence Jarvie (1968) (chief executive officer of the Flint Board of Education and general superintendent of community education). President Charles Donnelly (1968) of the junior college also supports this view, although adding that "the official position of the Flint Board of Education at this time is one matter, and that the official position of the superintendent [Jarvie] at the time agreed with the position of the Flint Board and this did not reflect the position of the Junior College faculty or of the Junior College administration."

Toward the end of 1962, several events appear to have coalesced the Flint residents' feelings that a change in the Flint College structure would be beneficial. Earlier that year, Jarvie had come to Flint from New York City. "I hadn't been there very long until I made a couple of conclusions with regard to higher education, not only in Flint, but in the State of Michigan," Jarvie (1968) has stated. "It appeared to me inevitable that the State of Michigan had to have another University Center. . . . The natural location, after I looked at the state as a whole, was in the Flint area." Other Flint residents, such as J. A. Anderson—who had served on the original Citizen's Committee in the early fifties—viewed the expansion of the public system of education through the creation of new state-supported universities (see Chapter Five) as a potential threat to Flint, which, although the first Michigan community to secure a branch campus, might now be left with only an upper division institution while other communities developed university centers.

The first public statement regarding the possible expansion of the Flint program came on November 8, 1962, when Niehuss addressed a conference of principals and freshman counselors at Ann Arbor. "University centers at Flint and Dearborn offer opportunity for expansion," Niehuss said in discussing the need to handle rapidly increasing demands for college education across the state, "and it seems certain that these centers will have to consider extending their offerings to the freshman and sophomore years" (cited by *Flint Journal*, 1962a). When asked for comment, George Gundry, president of the Flint Board of Education, stated that although the board had not formally discussed this possibility, "members, as individuals, have expressed great interest in the possibility of expanding the U. of M.'s Flint program" (cited by *Flint Journal*, 1962a).

According to Niehuss (1968), the newspaper article reporting his speech did not quote him correctly, although "I did point out . . . that it had been suggested that since we have these campuses, there was the possibility that they could be extended to four-year colleges, and also there was the possibility that the community colleges throughout the state might extend to four years." Moreover, the first informal approach to the university had already taken place the previous month when, according to Niehuss, he had been approached by Jarvie and Charles Stewart Mott at the dedication of the new joint library facility. "Would you consider, now that we've got this nice library here," Niehuss recalls Jarvie's asking, "extending the University of Michigan's two years to four years?" Niehuss replied that although the university was eager to develop the present relations to their fullest, he would have no objection to discussing other possible arrangements.

On December 17, 1962, representatives of the University of Michigan were invited to a dinner meeting in Flint by Frank Manley of the Mott Foundation on behalf of Mott. In addition to Manley, Mott, and the university representatives (Niehuss, French, and Harold Dorr), Jarvie and others associated with the junior college and with the Flint Board of Education joined the meeting, at which time Mott raised the question of university interest in expanding the Flint unit to a four-year program. Both French and Niehuss received the impression that Mott would be willing to offer financial support for construction of an expanded institution in Flint. By the end of the evening, a joint committee of Flint residents (Jarvie, Roy Brownell, a trustee of the Mott Foundation, and Guy J. Bates, a member of the Flint Board of Education) and university personnel (Niehuss, French, and Dorr) had been created "to explore in depth the future of higher education in the Flint area."

The committee deliberations and study continued over most of the following year, and not until February 12, 1964, was the first report made to the Flint Board of Education. On that date, the

Bates Committee, as the joint committee was then known, presented its findings regarding the future of higher education in the Flint area—or, more correctly, regarding the future of Flint College. Based on projections of future demands from a seven-county "Flint metropolitan area," the committee concluded that "present opportunities for college study, especially at the lower division level, are limited in scope, and that the over-all program is wanting in emphases and in diversification." Moreover, "it [the committee] is convinced that a hyphenated four-year program does not and cannot adequately serve the educational needs of the seven-county area." Because of the expanding need (created, in part, by basing the study on a larger geographic area than that which the municipal junior college was serving) and the implied failures of the existing upper division institution in Flint, the committee then recommended that the Flint Board of Education invite the University of Michigan to develop a four-year college in Flint at the earliest possible date (Bates, 1964, pp. 14–15).

The one interested party not directly represented on the Bates Committee—and the institution most adversely affected by the recommendation—was Flint Community Junior College, for which Jarvie and Gundry had acted as spokesmen. Despite the committee recommendation (Bates, 1964, p. 18) that all parties announce an intent "to preserve the identity, character and purposes of the two institutions," a decision to expand Flint College would, of necessity, modify the character and identity of the community college, especially since all parties, including Donnelly, agreed that the community college should expand its occupational and vocational offerings in view of the changing educational needs in Flint during the late 1950's and early 1960's. Yet, Donnelly (1968) felt that the occupational (nontransfer) offerings could be expanded under existing administrative and organizational arrangements; moreover, he felt that an expansion of Flint College into the freshman and sophomore years might force the community college too deeply into occupational education, the only area in which it would not be competing for students with the university branch.

On the other hand, Jarvie was strongly in favor of greatly increasing the community college nontransfer functions. Representatives of the university were somewhat apprehensive of the effect a shift in community college emphasis might have on the already limited number of juniors transferring from the community college to Flint College. Although "we didn't feel that the experiment had been a failure . . . [and] I think that I would say that educationally it seemed to be good," Niehuss (1968) felt that a decision to shift the community college emphasis toward vocational offerings would require reconsideration of a single four-year unit—which the university had supported as early as 1952—from which a steady supply of sophomores qualified for junior standing at Flint College could be assured.

Jarvie also felt that the community college could continue a strong although lessened emphasis on its liberal arts transfer programs despite a four-year university branch in Flint. Although community college officials greatly feared direct competition with an expanded Flint College for students planning to transfer, Jarvie thought such competition would not occur because Flint Community Junior College could continue to offer lower tuition for residents of Flint, while allowing the university to offer lower tuition for other residents of the seven-county area.

Above all, Jarvie, Anderson, and other representatives of the Flint community—as opposed to the community college—were concerned with the status of Flint relative to other communities in the state which were securing four-year colleges and universities as part of the expansion of the state-supported system of higher education during the late fifties and early sixties. This expansion, which was also partially responsible for the university decision in the fifties to develop branch campuses to strengthen its own position in the state as a whole, threatened to leave Flint in the position of a trail breaker outpaced. Thus, although a desire to "protect" Flint Community Junior College had been central to the 1952 Flint decision to reject the university offer of a full four-year program, by 1964 other considerations prevailed.

The Flint Board of Education took formal action on the Bates Report at its April 8 meeting. After noting the "importance of the establishment of a four-year college working with the existing two-year college to provide a broad scope of educational opportunity beyond high school not only for the citizens of the School District of the City of Flint, but also for the natural Flint metropolitan area," the Board voted that "as representatives of the citizens of the City of Flint, [the Board] warmly invites the Board of Regents of the University of Michigan to establish a four-year college in the City of Flint within the structure of the recommendations transmitted." Those recommendations, also drawn from the Bates Report, were primarily concerned with academic standards and fiscal relationships, neither of which would provide any problems in discussions with university officials.

The response to the resolution was predictable. On the one hand, members of the community college faculty and staff who, according to the *Flint Journal* (1964), "have expressed the only public opposition to the expansion plan" continued to press for more study and discussion, despite Bates's appeal that they "lay aside their opposition to the proposal and offer constructive cooperation instead" and the Board of Education (1964) resolution which "recognized the important role of Flint Community Junion College in higher education" and promised "that appropriate representatives of Flint Community Junior College will be involved in all planning with respect to the evolution of programs in higher education and that the role of Flint Community Junior College will be an inherent part of any programs which will be developed."

The Board of Regents, on the other hand, reacted quickly and favorably. Noting the increasing enrollment pressures on the university and commenting that "the success of this operation [Flint College] has been gratifying," the regents moved to "accept the principle of the proposed cooperative program and express their concurrence with the views of the Flint Board of Education that the educational needs of the Flint area as well as those of the state would be well served by extending the present program of the Flint College of The University of Michigan" (University of Michigan, 1966, pp. 303–304). The regents also agreed that Flint Community Junior College had an important role to play in providing for diverse educational opportunities in the Flint area and requested the cooperation of the faculty and staff of the junior college in the development of new plans for Flint College. Finally, the regents

instructed the administration of the university to "proceed as ex-
peditiously as possible" to open the expanded program by September 1965.

For all practical purposes, the decision to end the upper
division-only organization at Flint College had been taken, although
a combination of politics and power struggles provided a period of
confusion and potential delay until the expanded program began
admitting freshmen, as requested by the regents, in September 1965.
Throughout the summer, meetings were held among faculty members of Flint College and Flint Community Junior College to make
recommendations. They reached agreement on several points concerning curriculum and cooperation. The university publicly announced on October 5, 1964, that it would admit a freshman class
of 200 at Flint the following September.

During this same period, the university included appropriations for the expanded Flint program in its budget request for the
coming fiscal year. Yet, the new program was suddenly embroiled
in a political and jurisdictional power struggle involving the newly
created State Board of Education, which moved in late 1964 to review the plans for Flint, despite the fact that "discussions on expansion of the Flint College were initiated at the invitation of the Flint
community more than two years before the new State Constitution
[under which the board had been created] became effective" (University of Michigan, 1965). On January 15, 1965, as pressure continued to build, Mott publicly announced his offer of $2.4 million
for construction of the facilities required for the expanded program,
which would continue to share campus, library, and other facilities
with the junior college. The following month, in part because of
legislative pressure resulting from the competition for new state institutions, which had also motivated Flint, Governor George Romney asked a delay in planning and submitted his own budget request
without including the money for expansion. Concurrently, hearings
were announced by the State Board of Education and the Appropriations Committee of the state senate.

The State Board of Education published its position paper,
requesting the university to abandon plans for an expanded Flint
College, in April 1965. Thomas J. Brennan, president of the board,

sent a copy of the report to President H. A. Hatcher on May 20, 1965, expressing "regret that the press of so many duties prevented it [the State Board] from providing this document to you at a sooner time." Although the intent of this gesture was not lost on university officials, the situation by that time was beyond the control of the State Board of Education, which had no legal power to force university compliance. Under increasing pressure from supporters of the university, legislators from Flint, and other proponents of local autonomy, Romney had privately reversed his position and had let it be known that he would support the expansion of Flint College (Niehuss, 1968). With this assurance and with the inclusion of the necessary funds in the final budget approved in June, the university opened its expanded institution in September 1965.

The initial enrollment of 835 students at the expanded institution seemed to bear out many of the assumptions on which the expansion was based; although the figure included only freshmen, juniors, and seniors, it was almost 200 students above that of the previous year and represented the largest single increase in enrollment since the inception of the institution. Moreover, the student body was drawn from a larger geographic area than before and included many more students from the "Flint metropolitan area" than had formerly attended Flint College. By the following academic year, 1966–1967, enrollment had again increased so that, in its first year of operation as a full four-year institution, Flint College enrolled 919 students. By the fall of 1968, enrollment had again climbed to an all-time high of 1,967, of whom approximately 75 per cent were full-time students.

In 1954, when Flint College was created as an upper division institution, the University of Michigan had favored a unified program, whether or not the junior college maintained its separate legal identity. The community, on the other hand, had supported the idea of a completely separate institution, partially because of local pride in the junior college and partially because of financial and legal considerations involving a trust fund tied to the junior college. The ultimate university decision, based upon assumptions of adequate enrollment and cooperation, was to accept the local offer—which included monetary support for new facilities—and to generalize this action into a statement of policy which was then applied to the Dearborn situation and later to Flint again: The university would provide educational offerings where a community demonstrated both need and a desire for such services, as well as a willingness to offset the costs of facilities and initial maintenance.

By 1962, French still felt that "in general, there was good cooperation between the Flint College and F.C.J.C." Although the 1954 assumptions concerning enrollment had been proven wrong, size alone would not have prompted the university to expand its program without the initiative of the Flint community. This initiative, based on a desire to have a full four-year college (or university center) in Flint, was accepted by the university not because of any flaw in the original assumptions concerning Flint College but because the 1954 events had "happened as an historical accident, not as a deliberate attempt to demonstrate a new educational structure" (French, 1966). The university was not committed to Flint College as an educational or experimental unit; it had developed because circumstances and community pressure so dictated. When circumstances and community desires changed, Flint College changed with them.

By the time the university Board of Regents had decided to institute a freshman and sophomore program at Flint College, three upper division institutions (Dearborn College, Concordia Senior College, and the New School College) were in operation, while two more (Florida Atlantic University and the University of West Florida) had been approved. The following year, when Flint admitted its first freshman class, another upper division institution, Richmond College, was approved, and three more new programs were developed within the next two years. What had begun, at College of the Pacific and the New School, as an educational experiment based on theories of secondary-preparatory–university organization was now essentially a pragmatic response to the growing numbers of community college graduates.

Seven

The New Wave

The City University of New York—the municipal, tuition-free system of higher education in New York City—was established upon recommendation of the board of the old Municipal College System, the Board of Higher Education, by an act of the New York State legislature in the spring of 1961. At the time of its creation, the new university already included seven institutions (four four-year colleges and three community colleges) enrolling over 97,000 students. The oldest of these colleges was City College, founded as the Free Academy in 1847; the newest, Queensborough Community College, had been established in 1958 and had admitted its first class in the fall of 1960. Also in 1961, the Board of Higher Education retained Thomas C. Holy to be a special consultant and to develop for the already existing board Committee to Look to the

129

Future a report which would be used as a basis for further long-range planning as was required under New York State law.

Holy's study, completed in May 1962 and transmitted to the Board of Higher Education on June 18, 1962, made extensive recommendations for both the improvement and the expansion of the City University structure. Noting that "at present, each borough in the City has a Senior College campus except Richmond [Staten Island]," Holy recommended that "very shortly, the Board of Higher Education initiate a detailed study of the need for a Senior College to serve the Borough of Richmond, and that as a part of that study consideration be given to the feasibility of developing a Senior College on the same or adjoining site of the Staten Island Community College, and thus permit joint use of certain common facilities, such as auditorium and gymnasium" (Board of Higher Education of New York City, 1962, pp. 347–348).

When the Holy Committee recommended consideration of a senior college on Staten Island, it did not imply an upper division institution similar to Concordia Senior College; within the City University of New York, four-year institutions were traditionally known as senior colleges as opposed to the two-year, or community, colleges. Furthermore, the idea of a four-year institution on Staten Island was not new. Community sentiment on the island had long been in favor of it, and Professor Arleigh B. Williamson, soon after his appointment to the Board of Higher Education in August 1954, had begun to push for the creation of such an institution. After sounding out various members of the board and representatives of the State Education Department and the city government, Williamson (1968) decided "that the expeditious thing to do was to get a foot inside the door toward complete higher education and that foot in the door would be a community college." Yet, the idea remained that at some future date, the proposed community college could and would be expanded to a four-year institution.

Following the establishment of the community college, which opened with 117 students in the fall of 1956, Williamson "let the thing lie fallow," although Peter Spiridon, a faculty member at the college and later survey director of the studies leading to the establishment of Richmond College, has stated (1968) that even in

1955 and 1956, "some of the hiring done here at the college was
based on the assumption that we might eventually become a four-
year college." By 1962, after the publication of the Holy Report,
Williamson (1968) felt that "the time seemed to be ripe that we
could advance this need, explore and make evident this need for a
four-year college." Thus, on December 17, 1962, the Board of
Higher Education (1963, pp. 671–672) announced "the appointment of an appropriate committee [chaired by Williamson, who
had also chaired the committee which established the community
college] to give special consideration to the possible development of
the Staten Island Community College into a four year college."

Almost immediately, consideration of expanding the community college came under heavy fire from representatives of the
State University of New York (of which all New York State community colleges—even those within the City University—are a part)
and from the State Board of Regents. Although neither the regents
nor the trustees of the State University were then on record as
opposing conversion of community colleges, State University Vice
President Boyd Golder informed Williamson that "the State was not
going to permit community colleges to develop into four-year colleges" (Williamson, 1968). By March 18, 1963, the Board of
Higher Education (1964c, p. 17) was no longer speaking in terms
of conversion but rather of "exploration of the need for establishing
a four-year program in the Borough of Richmond leading to a baccalaureate degree"; by September of that same year, the Williamson committee was officially known as the Committee to Explore
the Need for Establishing a Four-Year Program in the Borough of
Richmond.

On November 10, 1963, the committee formally launched
a survey, in cooperation with civic, industrial, and educational leaders on Staten Island, to establish the need for a four-year program
in addition to that being offered by the local community college.
According to S. V. Martorana (1968), university dean for two-
year colleges at the State University of New York, an article in
The Staten Island Advance reporting the beginning of the survey
was "the first written notice this office had concerning the 'need for
a four-year city college on Staten Island.' " On December 20, 1963,

Paul Orvis, Martorana's predecessor, wrote to Gustave G. Rosenberg, then chairman of the Board of Higher Education. Although "we are not aware of the full facts of the situation and realize that much of this publicity is a result of statements by certain Staten Island public officials and not by City University," Orvis wrote, "our Trustees have been concerned over several newspaper reports with regard to the potential conversion of the Staten Island Community College to a four year college at that location." Orvis never stated that the regents or trustees would not approve such a conversion; he did, however, request "a statement from your Board together with any studies that might have been made to indicate your long range plans for the present community college."

Rosenberg's reply (1964), "after several conferences concerning the content of your letter . . . and following discussions with Professor Arleigh B. Williamson," was direct and to the point. Rosenberg stated unequivocally "that we have never changed nor do we intend to change the use or purpose of the two-year community college as it is at present. We intend in good faith to go through with our program of construction of the Staten Island Community College with no thought of converting same to a four-year program. . . . To sum up, it is the clear intent of this Board that the two-year college in Staten Island continue in the future as a two-year institution."

Apparently, Staten Island Community College was not the only two-year college in the state which had been considered by local sponsors as a possible base for a four-year college. According to Martorana (1968), "hints of a wish to escalate from a two-year to a four-year college had come from other quarters as well." Following the correspondence between Orvis and Rosenberg, the State University moved to establish a policy with regard to conversion. The 1964 State University Master Plan stated "that, for the foreseeable future, no existing two-year college be expanded into a four-year college"; the Board of Regents repeated and endorsed the same statement in 1964 (University of the State of New York, 1965, p. 32). By 1966, the statement had been expanded to read: "Two-year and four-year colleges, in a planned, coordinated, and complete system of public higher education, provide essential and complementary, but distinctive, services in post-high-school education. Therefore, existing 2-year colleges should not be converted to 4-year baccalaureate college status as an approach to the expansion of college programs in any region in the State" (cited by Board of Higher Education of New York City, 1967, p. 61).

The initial considerations at Staten Island, coupled with other "hints" from throughout the state, had led the State University to believe that a concrete statement of policy was required; yet, given Williamson's conversations with Golder and Rosenberg's correspondence with Orvis, the regents' statements were no longer necessary to ensure the existing two-year status of Staten Island Community College. By the time the first regents' statement was published (April 1965), planning at the City University had progressed from conversion through consideration of a full four-year institution to the first draft of a paper which proposed creation of an upper division institution. According to Williamson (1968), the initial response of the state had "stopped us cold in our tracks. . . . Our presumption when we started this survey [November 10, 1963] was that we would have to establish a new four-year college."

Williamson's report to the Board of Higher Education (1965a), presented on September 30, 1964, outlined the results of the survey begun ten months earlier under the direction of Spiridon. After detailing the past and projected population growth on the island and its impact on high school and college enrollments, the report cited evidence of students' willingness, as well as need, to attend a four-year institution in Richmond. Present high school students in lower Brooklyn and Manhattan, as well as in Staten Island, were polled, as were teachers on Staten Island who might want to return to school for postgraduate study. These polls, according to the report, demonstrated increasing need for a public institution offering baccalaureate education on Staten Island, not only for those presently attending college in other boroughs of the city but also for those who, for lack of a public institution, were not attending college at all (pp. 1–3, 19, 22–31).

Williamson's recommendation, approved in principle by the board, was "the establishment in the Borough of Richmond, as a part of the City University of New York, [of] a four-year college, on the pattern of its other senior colleges" (Board of Higher Education of New York City, 1964a, p. 31). According to both Spiridon (1968) and Williamson (1968), the basic goal of the committee was to determine the need for a four-year college on the island, and they fully expected that a four-year institution would then be established because, as Williamson has stated, "we saw no other way to do it" since the state had eliminated the option of converting the community college. Yet, some members of the board challenged the idea of a full four-year college which would compete with the community college, and on December 21, 1964, a new committee was created which, according to Williamson, was "to describe how it could be done."

The report of the second Williamson committee, often referred to as the implementation committee, was submitted to the board and adopted on June 21, 1965. At that time, the board approved "the creation and establishment in the Borough of Richmond, as part of The City University of New York (as an implementation of its September 30, 1964 resolution, Item No. 3), of an 'upper-division' college consisting of the third and fourth college years" (Board of Higher Education of New York City, 1966, pp. 257–258). The new report, building on the need for a four-year program demonstrated in the September 30, 1964, document, included a survey of City University community college students' interest in attending such an institution, as well as a brief discussion of other upper division institutions, in Florida and Michigan, which were presented as examples of how such an institution could operate successfully.

Williamson has stated (1968) that during the early stages of the preparation of the implementation report, "it dawned on us that we could establish two years despite the community college— without the community college"—and that this realization provided the germ of the idea for an upper division institution on Staten Island. The basic concept of an upper division institution, however, had already appeared in the 1964 City University Master Plan (1964a), prepared by Dean Harry L. Levy. This document, published in November 1964, included a section entitled "Guide-Lines for the Second Quadrennium, 1968–72." Item 1 was a statement of the need for "a publicly-supported senior college on Staten Island," while, on the same page, Item 3, titled "Upper Division College," stated that "serious consideration is being given to establishing one of the new senior colleges with a very small freshman and sophomore class or with none at all" (pp. 79–80).

Levy "became aware of the upper-division college movement through conversations in 1963 with my fellow-members of the Steering Committee of the Social Studies and Humanities Curriculum Program of the American Council of Learned Societies and Educational Services Incorporated, at least one of whom came from Florida, where the experiment was being launched" (1968). As early as April 14, 1964—three months before the completion of Williamson's first report—Levy (1964) had presented the paragraph on upper division institutions to the Administrative Council (Council of Presidents) of the university for approval and inclusion in the Master Plan. Neither Levy nor Williamson had yet connected the Staten Island and upper division statements in his own mind. "I was aware of that [the Master Plan statement]," Williamson (1968) has said, "but it had not occurred to us, when the first report came out, that this might be the expedient thing to do."

On September 1, 1964, E. K. Fretwell came to the City University from the State Education Department as dean for academic development; he may have been the first person to connect the upper division concept with the planning for Richmond County. Fretwell had been coauthor of the 1956 and 1957 regents' statements in which the idea of an upper division institution had first received public support in New York State (see Chapter Five). Now, upon arrival at the City University, he discovered that "it was generally conceded around 80th Street [City University administrative offices] that it [the idea of an upper division institution] was an excellent idea" (Fretwell, 1968). Thus, although he did not introduce the idea to the City University, Fretwell was pleased to note its currency and began "to make sure that in any documentation coming out of the City University reference was made to a bachelor's degree granting institution" rather than to a four-year college. On November 11, 1964, Fretwell wrote to Chancellor Albert Bowker, "I am convinced that we should plan for an upper division college for Staten Island. . . . My conversation with Professor Williamson yesterday (I took the initiative for talking with him) convinces me that there is pretty good general agreement as to what we're aiming for."

The following week, Fretwell left New York to investigate new developments in community colleges and upper division colleges; during the next six weeks he visited Washington, Miami, Detroit, Chicago, and California, as well as Florida Atlantic University and Dearborn College. The visits had originally been planned while Fretwell was with the State Education Department as part of a six-month sabbatical study of new developments in higher education to be supported by the Carnegie Corporation. He was forced to limit both the scope and duration of his study, although the trip had developed new practical implications: an opportunity to study at firsthand existing upper division institutions.

Fretwell, Levy, and Williamson met on January 21, 1965, to discuss the results of Fretwell's visits, and on January 22, Fretwell sent Williamson a set of documents he had collected during his trip. In the covering letter (1965a), Fretwell called Williamson's attention to the 1956 and 1957 regents' statements of support for the idea (which had recently been repeated in the 1964 statewide plan) and to the eight "Advantages of the Community College-Senior College Plan" included in the 1957 statement. Florida Atlantic University, Fretwell wrote, was experiencing some enrollment difficulties, but he attributed them "to the commuter travel distance from Miami-Dade Junior College and the lack of dormitories as yet at Boca Raton" rather than to any inherent weakness in the concept of an upper division institution. Fretwell also noted the decision to add freshmen and sophomores at Flint (which he had visited in 1962, although not on his more recent trip) "as a result of statewide enrollment pressures." Nonetheless, "the senior college will probably have more juniors than freshmen for some time to come" and should not be viewed as a complete rejection of the upper division concept.

By the middle of February, Spiridon's studies of need and acceptance were well under way, and Fretwell sent Spiridon—at Williamson's request—a draft of the sections which were to follow the survey results in the final report. In response to the rhetorical question "Why an upper division college?" Fretwell (1965b) gave eight reasons, several of which were similar to those originally listed in the 1957 regents' statement. Such an institution, according to Fretwell, would refrain from duplicating existing programs on Staten Island; would make possible upper division opportunities sooner than if a new institution were started, class by class, with the freshman year; would provide a high quality student body since community colleges would screen out uncapable students; would, at the same time, provide opportunities for "late bloomers" whose potential was recognized only after admission to the community college; would strengthen the master's degree by linking it more closely to the baccalaureate in an institution which could concentrate on upper division and master's study (shades of David Jordan and Robert Hutchins); would make effective use of resources through a partnership with the community college; would draw stronger faculty through the promise of only junior, senior, and graduate instructional responsibilities; and would provide for a relevant and immediate tailoring of offerings to the needs of the local community.

Although Williamson has stated (1968) that "except by rumor, the members [of the Board of Higher Education] did not know until the June release that the Committee had given up the earlier projected full four-year college and were to advocate the 'upper division,'" Fretwell had, as early as February 25, 1965, presented a report to the Administrative Council on "a proposal that the baccalaureate-granting college recommended for Staten Island by Board of Higher Education action on 9/30/64, consist of the junior and senior years, together with a one year master's degree for those who wish to go on" (City University of New York, 1965). On April 15, 1965, the first draft of the Williamson implementation report (Board of Higher Education of New York City, 1965c) was complete, including the Fretwell draft of February 12, the results of the Spiridon surveys, and a number of proposed curricula based on the expressed needs of Staten Island business and civic leaders, as well as the opinions of Walter Willig, president of Staten Island Community College, and other educators in the city.

One more step remained before the proposal could be

brought before the Board of Higher Education. Bowker wrote to the State Education Department, informing it of the proposed creation of an upper division institution and requesting clarification of funding formulas under existing legislation. In addition, Bowker requested that the state notify New York City Mayor Robert Wagner of its approval of this concept, along with appropriate assurance with respect to funding. Wagner had already, on October 21, 1964, pledged "my Administration's support of such a vital education project" (cited by Board of Higher Education of New York City, 1965b, p. 483) following the first Williamson report. On June 3, 1965, Deputy Commissioner of Education Ewald B. Nyquist wrote to Wagner giving his support to the proposed institution. "The Regents have for a decade advocated the establishment of upper division institutions offering at least the baccalaureate degree," Nyquist wrote (1965), sending "assurances of our full endorsement of the proposed development and our deep appreciation of the willingness shown by the City University to initiate this innovation and constructive change."

On June 21, 1965, the final report of the Williamson Committee to Explore the Need for Establishing a Four-Year Program in the Borough of Richmond (Board of Higher Education of New York City, 1965a) was presented to the Board of Higher Education. The June report, as approved by the board, included no basic changes from the April 15 draft except that three pages, including the citation from the 1964 regents' plan and the proposed resolutions, had been moved from before the survey reports to the end of the document. Following passage of the resolution to create the new institution, Rosenberg (cited by *New York Times,* 1965) characterized the new college as "pioneering in the state with a creative means of carrying out our policy of expanding educational opportunity."

Publicly, the new college was hailed as a creative response to the needs of the city; privately, however, officials emphasized other factors. Fretwell, who had come to the City University with "a series of preconceptions and discovered . . . that the preconceptions actually fitted the situation," has stated (1968) that "the aim . . . was to keep the community college from switching over and becoming a four-year college." His trips reinforced his views that this might be a good idea, although "if the other ones hadn't existed we would have come up with the same results anyway." Furthermore, although his trips did represent a significant attempt to learn from other institutions, he incorrectly assumed that there were no other such colleges in the northeast and that "Florida is so well pleased with the upper-division college idea that a second is now planned for Pensacola" (cited by Board of Higher Education of New York City, 1965a, p. 7). In fact, the New School College had then been in operation for two decades in New York, while the Pensacola institution was approved before Florida Atlantic had admitted its first class.

Williamson's first intention, dating back to the early fifties, was to convert the local junior college; only when this option was blocked by the State Education Department did he begin to consider a full four-year institution. When this alternative was questioned by other members of the Board of Higher Education, the second Williamson committee determined how a four-year institution could be created without overly threatening the existing community college. The final decision to create an upper division institution "was an expedient; we thought that if we could do this, if it was practicable to do this, if there were antecedents to do this, or if we could work the matter out in practical terms, this would serve as an expedient for not making the Staten Island Community College a four year college. It was only after we began to work on this, to implement this expediency, that we discovered that this had virtues in itself" (Williamson, 1968). Despite the statement in Williamson's June 1965 report that both Florida Atlantic University and Dearborn College were "institutions [that] appear to be in a dynamic growth situation," Williamson later stated (1968) that "this had not been tried out sufficiently any place else to serve as a true precedent."

The creation of Richmond College, not unlike the creation of the Florida or Michigan institutions, was the result of a converging set of needs and circumstances, including the need for additional baccalaureate degrees and the existence of a local community, or junior, college. Although Staten Island Community College was created in 1956 to get "a foot in the door" when Staten Island had no public institution of higher education, by 1964 the circumstances mitigated against providing a four-year program. By that time, the state position on conversion of two-year institutions had been developed, and members of the Board of Higher Education were not willing to accede to Williamson's desire for establishment of a four-year institution at the possible expense of the existing community college. Ultimately, Richmond College was the result of both educational and political pressure to provide four years of public higher education on Staten Island and was, at least indirectly, "made necessary by the great growth of junior colleges in the period that followed World War II" (*New York Times,* 1965).

During the same period that the City University was developing Richmond College, Pratt Institute in Brooklyn, New York, was also moving toward creation of a "senior college," although, according to Richard H. Heindel (1968), then president of Pratt, "it was never contemplated that the Pratt Senior College would appeal to a large number of students, such as the possible transfer students from community colleges." In fact, Pratt Senior College was basically a device through which Pratt Institute could "inject more liberal arts into our particular artistic environment" and provide the opportunity for both a strengthened liberal arts component and the offering, to a limited number of Pratt students, of a liberal arts degree.

Prior to this time, Pratt Institute was known principally for its programs in art, design, architecture, and engineering, in addition to its library school and division of fashion design. Liberal arts courses required for the professional programs—Pratt gave no liberal arts degrees—were offered through the Division of General Studies. In late 1963, Louis Sass, dean of the Library School, suggested to Heindel the possibility of creating a two-year undergraduate program with a liberal arts orientation to feed into the existing master's program in library science. The proposed arrangement according to Sass (1963), "would attract graduates of two-year community colleges who might wish to transfer to Pratt for a three-year course of study that would combine an undergraduate major in English, Social Studies, Mathematics, Chemistry, or Physics and a graduate major in Library Science."

Heindel's reaction was entirely favorable, although he looked beyond specific offerings in library science to "some exciting opportunities for upper-level work by the Division of General Studies" (Heindel, 1964a) which Sass's proposal suggested. Heindel had been particularly impressed with the example of M.I.T. after the Second World War, in which the humanities had been successfully integrated into "a heavily scientific and technical atmosphere," and had been searching for a means of accomplishing a similar integration at Pratt. As early as May 5, 1962, he stated in his inaugural address that "it is psychologically and socially sound to combine liberal and professional education. . . . But we do not need to underwrite the whole apparatus." Heindel felt that secondary education was increasingly able to accomplish the job of general education. "Whatever we add . . . will be in the third and fourth or fift year curriculums, so that we build upon what the students are bringing, and truly operate at the collegiate level" (Heindel, 1962).[1]

On January 8, 1964, the major administrative officers and department chairmen met with Heindel to discuss Sass's proposal for an extended library program; by the end of the meeting, the proposal had been expanded to include a number of liberal arts programs, and the idea for Pratt Senior College was born. Heindel requested those present to consider the requirements—primarily in terms of additional courses and expense—which would have to be met to offer degree programs in certain liberal arts fields. By mid-March, discussions centered on possible majors in humanities or social sciences, which were considered to have the greatest drawing power and desirability with the least need for adding new courses (particularly languages) not already offered at Pratt. According to Ransom Noble (1968), then dean of the Division of General Studies and now dean of the Senior College, "it seemed sensible not to limit it to people who might want to go on to the library school,"

[1] By 1962, the "college" was well enough established as an institution of "higher education" that Heindel could refer to college level where Henry Tappan or William Harper would surely have stated university level.

especially since "every year we did have some Pratt students who found that they were in the wrong place and that they really belonged in liberal arts, although they might not necessarily want library science."

During May 1964 a number of "outsiders," including Frank Bowles of the Ford Foundation, Nyquist, deputy commissioner of education and head of the Middle States Association team that had visited Pratt, Frederick H. Jackson of the Carnegie Corporation, John Burchard of M.I.T., and Richard Cyert from Carnegie Tech were invited to Pratt to discuss the proposed senior college program (Noble, 1968). Noble prepared a confidential draft proposal (Noble and Sass, 1964a) for the senior college program for discussion with the visitors, outlining the two areas of concentration (humanities and social sciences) and the three groups the college would be designed to serve: junior college transfers, students interested in librarianship, and "students in the professional schools at Pratt who wish to transfer to a liberal arts major." At present, Noble wrote, "all we can do for such students is to give them a program of liberal arts for at most a year until they can effect transfer to another institution." Creation of a senior college program would permit these students "to complete their education at the Institute where they have developed friendships, loyalties, and interests"; it would also preserve approximately forty tuition-paying students each year who might otherwise leave Pratt in the middle of the program of studies.

On September 28, 1964, Heindel forwarded a revised draft (Noble and Sass, 1964b) of Noble's proposal to the Education Committee of the Board of Trustees, noting that "this modest but significant proposition" was designed to rename the Division of General Studies the School of Humanities and Social Science and to include within it Pratt Senior College (Heindel, 1964b). The Board of Trustees discussed and approved the proposal at its October 13, 1964, meeting, following Heindel's assurance that "with the exception of one or two courses, the proposal can be managed within the present budget" and that approval would be sought from Albany before any public announcements were made (Pratt Institute, 1964).

Discussions began the following week with Frank Hobson,

associate in higher education in the State Education Department, and continued through the following summer. Hobson's criticisms (1965) centered around two problems, as viewed from Albany: first, the broadly defined "majors" to be offered appeared to lack "a sequence based on some rationale and . . . a view toward eliminating duplication and proliferation"; second, the program was not designed to "accept almost any junior college graduate." Neither criticism caused Heindel concern since he "never felt many persons would come in from the two-year [public] community colleges because our tuition was relatively high." Furthermore, Pratt already had "a really sizable offering of liberal arts courses" and was interested in "a rearranging of the mechanics rather than anything else" (Heindel, 1968).

According to Noble (1969), "President Heindel's statement that Pratt was interested in 'a rearranging of the mechanics rather than anything else' doesn't represent the feelings that my faculty and I had about the Senior College. Certainly we shared his wish to strengthen the liberal arts content at Pratt. But we also hoped to attract a small but significant group of two-year college graduates. As far as we were concerned, the talk about these junior and community college students was not just for public consumption."

Under the new organization, put into effect in September 1966, "the School of Humanities and Social Science has two major responsibilities: first, to develop, administer, and teach the liberal arts courses included in the Institute's professional curricula; and second, through Pratt Senior College, to offer baccalaureate degrees in Humanities and Social Science" (Pratt Institute, 1966, p. 72). The student body of the senior college, which had "not yet conducted a major junior college recruitment campaign" (Noble, 1968), was composed in large part of former Pratt students who had taken advantage of the opportunity to change majors. Of the approximately sixty students in the first two classes of the senior college, no more than ten were junior college graduates.

The program at Pratt Institute, despite the name Pratt Senior College, is not that of an independent upper division institution; it lacks its own board, degrees, curricular offerings, administrative head (Noble is also dean of the College of Humanities and

Social Science, of which the senior college is a part), and geographical location. Pratt Senior College is of interest because of the comparisons one may make with other senior, or upper division, institutions in terms of the view of general, liberal, or professional education which each holds. In this sense, Pratt Senior College, more than most other upper division colleges established since 1950, was the result of some of the reasoning which led educators from Francis Wayland to Hutchins to question the basic organization of American higher education.

Pratt Senior College was not an outgrowth—as were Flint, Dearborn, Florida Atlantic, University of West Florida, and even Richmond—of the pressure of junior college transfers, industrial needs, or political decisions. In a manner somewhat similar to that at the New School in 1944, Pratt Senior College responded to internal needs, in this case the desire to strengthen one curriculum (library science) and to ensure opportunities for dissatisfied professional students to modify their program within Pratt Institute. As at the New School, the creation of an upper division program at Pratt did not involve large numbers of students or the addition of a significant number of new course offerings since the liberal arts core already existed for the professional (at Pratt) and graduate (at the New School) programs. Basically, all that was involved was a decision to allow students to take a number of core courses which led to a liberal arts degree.

Yet, the resulting senior college was definitely an upper division program operating at a truly collegiate level; Pratt was a professional school, and even the liberal arts offerings built upon the students' general education, which had already been completed. Thus, although a majority of the courses offered were identical to those taken by professional students to meet their general education requirements, the senior college program was designed to continue a student's preparatory work and to advance him from that point. In the case of the library science course, as at Richmond College, the last two years of college were consciously linked with the first year of graduate study (the master's degree) to create a truly university program.

The Pratt program, however similar, differed in one significant respect from that at the New School. In 1944, Alvin Johnson
and Hans Simons had seen the upper division college as an underpinning for a graduate program; the entire institution was still oriented toward "university programs," and the courses offered for the
baccalaureate degree were, in most cases, those also offered as part
of the graduate (or adult education) programs. At Pratt, on the
other hand, the senior college grew out of a concern for the undergraduate program, and the liberal arts majors were created as a
response to the needs of undergraduates. The resulting program,
with its reliance on courses also used as part of the undergraduate
liberal arts core, was still closely tied to the continuing general education offerings which a professional student might take at any
point within his undergraduate program. Thus, despite Heindel's
desire to create an upper-level program at Pratt Institute, he had
created a liberal arts program which happened to require two years
of study for admission, although the course content might have
been offered at any time within a four-year college program.

The potential educational weaknesses inherent in the creation of an "administrative" degree, as that at the New School had
been called, by a mere regrouping of existing courses to lead to a
baccalaureate, were not lost upon those involved in the development of Pratt Senior College. Yet, "as an alternative for our own
students," Noble has stated (1968), "it's worth doing [and] has
been a real service to them." President Simons at the New School
recognized these same weaknesses when, in the late fifties, he attempted to expand the New School Senior College to a four-year
program built upon a full-time instructional staff committed only
to this program. Yet, Simons' efforts failed (see Chapter Four),
and the New School Senior College remained virtually unchanged
until 1964, when a new administrative staff including Dean Allen
Austill and President John R. Everett came to the New School. One
of Everett's first acts was to make "an analysis of every program in
the institution and of its resource base [and] of its academic character and quality." One outcome of this analysis was the realization
that planning should begin "in terms of the possibilities of estab-

lishing a different kind of [baccalaureate] program—a program
that might be freer, that might be more truly undergraduate than
pre-graduate in its construction" (Everett, 1968).

Everett was not the first to discern serious weaknesses in the
existing baccalaureate program at the New School. As recently as
May 13, 1964, the Senior College Committee—itself composed of
part-time faculty teaching in the baccalaureate program—noted
that "for all practical purposes the present B.A. program is the simple accumulation of 120 credits provided these credits are distrib-
uted in a certain arbitrary fashion," that "the administration car-
ries the burden of the program rather than the faculty," and that
changes in the total New School offerings "are made in the best
interests of the adult non-credit student rather than the BA matricu-
lant" (New School, 1964, p. 2). These criticisms mirrored those
made eight years earlier by Simons and those made four years earlier during the successful attempt to secure accreditation from the
Middle States Association (1960, p. 11), which had noted that
"the basic elements of a 'major,' or of progression in a curriculum,
are not definite and clear." Yet no significant changes had been
made since the visit of the accreditation team nor, in fact, since
Simons' unsuccessful attempts to modify the program in 1957–1958.

The senior college at the New School had never enrolled
large numbers of students, and this had not been the original intent
(see Chapter Three). By 1960, after sixteen years in operation, the
program had graduated 409 students with the baccalaureate degree.
During the 1960–1961 academic year, the School of Politics and
the School of Philosophy and Liberal Arts offered 392 courses, enrolling over 5,480 students, of whom only 159 were registered for
baccalaureate credit. The original purpose of providing pregraduate
work for a small number of part-time adults was also being accomplished; in 1960, the average student was slightly over thirty-five
years old and required five years to complete the two-year program.
Thus, the program still served the purposes for which it had been
created; yet, by 1960, these purposes themselves were questioned.
The arrival of a new president and the naming of a new dean in
1964 provided the impetus to review and modify the purposes, pro-

cedures, and outcomes of the twenty-year-old baccalaureate program.

One of Everett's first acts, as stated above, was to review all aspects of the New School offerings, including but not limited to the baccalaureate program. Austill, who had been associate dean since August 1962, was already "quite dissatisfied with it [the baccalaureate program]" and had "decided that we should get out of this bachelor's degree program" (1968). A series of discussions took place among Austill, Everett, faculty, and students during the first months of Everett's presidency; one virtually unanimous conclusion was that the existing senior college should be abolished. On July 6, 1965, Everett outlined to the Board of Trustees his thinking on "a totally new conception and program [which] would be initiated" (Austill, 1965) to replace the existing baccalaureate program. The new program, for full-time students employing full-time faculty, would continue to admit students at the junior year; yet, like Simons' plan in the mid-fifties, it would be a day-time program to "be both economically and educationally productive."

Everett's proposal to the board was based on many of the factors which had led Simons, a decade earlier, to try to modify the New School Senior College. Because the physical plant was still underutilized during the day, a day college could be initiated for a small additional maintenance cost. A day program would imply a full-time student body and a full-time faculty, the latter a requirement if the program were not to suffer the same lack of supervision and of continuity which had weakened the old senior college. Everett did not have the same loyalties to the senior college emphasis on adult education which Johnson or Simons had; furthermore, many of those who had opposed Simons' reforms had now retired. Finally, Everett had his own specific ideas about what an innovative and creative college could offer "to meet the needs of bright students who find the conventional mass-production methods of liberal arts colleges uncongenial" (Austill, 1965).

The decision to continue with an upper division institution rather than to create a four-year program was based primarily on three considerations (Austill, 1968; Everett, 1968). First, creation of a lower division would require, as at Pratt, great expense because of the lack of existing facilities for lower division sciences or languages. Second, Everett and Austill felt that a significant population of highly qualified students were dropping out of "what traditionally have been called very good colleges" at the end of their sophomore years; these students could be attracted to an institution in New York City which offered a distinctive and "liberalizing" education. Finally, in addition to trying "to avoid the essential weaknesses of most 'good' liberal arts colleges, we also tried to incorporate a certain educational philosophy of what we thought was right"; this philosophy involved taking students with some prior education so that the New School offerings could lead "the student to begin to understand things in terms of meaningful interrelationships rather than just building blocks."

Following Everett's July presentation to the board, Austill spent the summer developing a proposal. Austill's September 8 memo to Everett incorporated much of the thinking described above; in addition, it outlined possible sequences of courses, divisional structures, and student body characteristics. On the basis of Austill's report, Everett agreed to hire two consultants, Harold Zyskind and Jay Williams, to develop syllabuses in the humanities and social sciences, respectively. The following month, Everett presented a status report to the Educational Policy Committee of the board, which reacted "enthusiastically in favor" (New School, 1965) of the proposal and recommended continued development of the plans for a new senior college.

Planning for the new program proceeded quickly, in part because "there was no one to defend the kind of educational program we were presently running at the baccalaureate level" (Austill, 1968). By early February 1966 the consultants' report had been completed, and comments had been received from a number of nationally known educators to whom the proposal had been sent. On February 4, 1966, the Educational Policy Committee again heard Everett explain the proposed program to replace "the present program [which], although offering a good education, does not have adequate quality control . . . [nor] a full-time faculty, and the degrees earned are therefore more administrative degrees than faculty degrees." The Educational Policy Committee recommended the new program for approval to the board, and the New School College was born. No action was ever taken to eliminate the old senior college; rather, a motion was approved to begin the new program in September 1966 (New School, 1966).

The New School College, a full-time, day-time upper division program, opened with sixty-four students in the fall of 1966; at the same time, approximately seventy-five students remained in the old senior college program, which was being phased out, with no new admissions as of February 1966. The revamped New School College failed, as did every program except those at Richmond and the University of West Florida, to meet its initial enrollment goal of 100 students, despite the fact that 169 applications were received. Yet, because the primary goal of the new program was quality, only seventy-one applicants had been accepted, and the "failure" to meet a projection made primarily to determine the required number of faculty was not considered serious. "We were surprised," Austill stated (1968), "to get so few [community college transfers] . . . but we weren't basing our planning on that assumption [that they would apply]." The planning had been correct in one major assumption: About half the new students were from New York City and had gone away to college before deciding to return to the New School program.

Thus, after twenty-two years of operation, the oldest existing upper division program ended, although it was replaced with a new upper division college, redesigned to meet the needs of the sixties. The New School College had been developed over a period of only eighteen months from Everett's advent as president to approval by the Board of Trustees; in this way, as in so many others, it was similar to Pratt Senior College, which had required only ten months, between January and October 1964, for its inception and approval. Each of these institutions received its first class in September 1966; at that same time, another upper division institution, the Capitol campus of the Pennsylvania State University, was also receiving its first class, a "token" group of eighteen students. Capitol campus had developed, as had Pratt and the New School, in a period of months; unlike the two New York City programs, however, Capitol campus was a result of external forces which created both pressures on and opportunities for Penn State to create a new institution in the Harrisburg area. The planning for Capitol campus was still incomplete upon the arrival of the first students and the first "real" class of 324 was not admitted until September 1967. Yet, technically, Capitol campus opened in 1966, making it the third program to open that year and the eighth upper division program then in operation.

The planning and development of the Capitol campus provide a striking example of a pragmatic response to a fluid situation, according to President Eric A. Walker of the Pennsylvania State University (1968). Prior to July 1965, the university had no intention of establishing an additional unit, let alone an upper division college, in or around Harrisburg, where it already cooperated with four other institutions in the operation of the Harrisburg Area Center for Adult Education (HACHE) and had, since earlier that year, offered master's degree programs in engineering through the Susquehanna Valley Graduate Center. Several private liberal arts colleges served the baccalaureate needs of the area, and the Harrisburg Area Community College, which had opened in 1964 as the first public community college established under the 1963 Pennsylvania community college law, already enrolled over 450 students.

Furthermore, in 1965 the entire structure of higher education in Pennsylvania, both public and private, was under review as the newly created (1963) State Board of Education continued its development of the first master plan for higher education. One significant issue still to be resolved was the future of the twenty commonwealth campuses, which Penn State operated. These campuses, all of which offered associate degree work and some of which offered "college parallel" programs, were most strongly opposed by supporters of the new public community colleges, who saw the existence of the commonwealth campuses as a definite threat to their growth. Partly as a result of this conflict, a consultants' report outlining the "elements of a master plan for the State" suggested in December 1965 that "no new two-year colleges or campuses should be established" by any group or institution until further study had been carried out and that existing commonwealth campuses should be encouraged to consider "some institutional status other than that of a Commonwealth Campus (such as an independent institution or as a Community College)" (Academy for Educational Development, 1965, pp. 49, 52).

This same consultants' report, while recognizing that "the expansion of higher education in the next 20 years can be expected to be so great that present institutions . . . will be unable to carry the load even after their expansion plans have been completed," recommended that "the future objectives of The Pennsylvania State University should include heavy emphasis on graduate and professional work" and that it "should expect to limit its freshman and sophomore enrollment even more rigorously than it does now and to accept substantially increased proportions of its juniors and seniors as transfer students" (pp. 44, 49). Penn State concurred in the judgment that it should "shift emphasis to the 'third and fourth year, graduate and professional training' it is unusually well equipped to provide" at its University Park campus (Administrative Committee on Long-Range Development, 1965, pp. 23–24); yet, it insisted that the Penn State system, including the commonwealth campuses—"this complex of established and accredited institutions"—would be the logical resource to use in meeting "the expanding need for two-year technical, and for baccalaureate and postgraduate, institutions" (Walker, 1965c, pp. 28–29).

Suddenly, in the midst of these developments, Governor William Scranton learned, in late July, that the Air Force was planning to close the Olmsted Air Force Base in Middletown, Pennsylvania, approximately ten miles southeast of Harrisburg. Almost immediately, Scranton contacted Walker to ask whether "it might be possible for Penn State to establish a graduate school which would utilize part of the Olmsted Air Force Base, and which might enhance the economy of the area" (cited by Walker, 1965b). Walker asked C. S. Wyand, chairman of the Administrative Committee on Long-Range Development, to prepare a proposal for the development of the Olmsted facilities, and on August 10, 1965, Wyand submitted a "confidential, preliminary working draft" to Walker. Wyand's report (Pennlyvania State University, 1965), which became the basic planning document for the new institution, recommended not simply a graduate school but an upper division college which could also offer associate degrees in selected technical areas in which it would have both the faculty and the facilities to provide the necessary courses.

On August 24, 1965, Walker wrote to Scranton outlining his thinking on the proposed Olmsted institution. A graduate school alone, Walker wrote, would not be large enough to support the necessary faculty and research; an undergraduate institution, which would make better use of the available facilities, would compete unnecessarily with other institutions in the area. An upper division and graduate institution, however, would complement the efforts of neighboring institutions, relieve some of the enrollment strain on the University Park campus, and allow for maximum utilization of faculty, classrooms, library, and laboratory equipment. Walker also reported that he had already discussed this proposal at a meeting with some of the "opinion formers" in Harrisburg and felt that "there is a large measure of acceptance of the idea." Furthermore, since the state wanted to demonstrate its capacity to utilize the available space at the earliest possible date, Walker assured Scranton that "we feel certain that if such a combination of programs were put together, it could be started in the fall of 1966 on a trial basis" (Walker, 1965b).

According to Walker (1968), the Capitol campus was not modeled on any existing institution but was the logical outgrowth of the factors cited in his letter to Scranton. By the end of August 1965 the basic decisions concerning the organization of the new institution had been made, dependent only upon approval by the Penn State trustees and the governor, and the willingness of the Department of Health, Education and Welfare, to whom title to the airport had been transferred, to release the property to the state for this purpose. Representatives of the local community college, including President Clyde Blocker and Bruce Cooper, chairman of the board, had been informed of the tentative plans at the August 16 meeting referred to by Walker in his letter to Scranton; although Walker correctly discerned that "there are some strained relations with Messrs. Blocker and Cooper that developed during the past year," Walker (1966a) felt that the new institution could "eventually establish a very wholesome working arrangement with the developing Community Colleges" despite the possibility of offering certain associate degree programs on the Olmsted campus. "It is not our intention in any way to compete with the HACC [Harrisburg Area Community College]," Walker wrote (1965a) on September 8, 1965, "but rather to better meet the educational needs of Central Pennsylvania."

In early October, both Scranton and Walker notified the Council of Higher Education—one of the two councils composing the State Board of Education—of the plans for the new institution, although Severino Stefanon, secretary to the board, has stated (1969) that "at no time did The Pennsylvania State University request approval from the State Board of Education for the establishment of the Capitol Campus" nor, under the general regulatory powers granted to the board, was such approval necessary. The board, at its October 14 meeting, took note of Walker's memorandums but "cited the complete lack of information available to the Council . . . [and], therefore, could not formulate any recommendation" at that time (State Board of Education of the Commonwealth of Pennsylvania, 1965a, p. 26-6).

By November 1, 1965, three weeks before the governor formally requested that the university become "the applying agent for the Commonwealth of Pennsylvania to secure portions of the Olmsted Air Force Base (North Complex) to be developed and used by the University as a higher education facility," word had spread at University Park that the university might "develop an upperclass and graduate institution at the former Olmsted Air Force Base," and at least one department, public administration, was beginning to develop curricula so that it could be represented at the new institution. On November 10, following a visit to the proposed site, the State Board of Education again considered the Olmsted proposals. Noting once again that the university had failed to submit any formal proposals for consideration, the board concluded nonetheless that the availability of the Olmsted site "may be a once-in-a-lifetime opportunity to aid higher education effectively and economically." Yet, the board was not convinced that the creation of an upper division institution would make best use of the land;

"there is a potential," the board reported, "for a new university here, which might be developed over a 10 to 15 year period." Although the board did not suggest "that all decision on the facility must await the completion and adoption of the Master Plan," it did note that this plan was still being developed and recommended "that a detailed outline of a plan for the conversion of the Olmsted Base into an educational institution should be submitted to the Council in detail while the Master Plan is being developed" (State Board of Education of the Commonwealth of Pennsylvania, 1965b, p. 27-7).

Although Walker had reported to the state board that "neither the University nor the Board of Trustees have made the educational and other policy decisions needed before an application or a plan can be prepared" (cited by State Board of Education of the Commonwealth of Pennsylvania, 1965b, p. 27-7), sufficient planning had been accomplished by November 29 to permit the submission to the university trustees' Executive Committee of a proposal which would authorize "the officers of the University" to develop detailed plans for "an academic program to be operated as an integral part of the University." This program, to be opened as a new commonwealth campus in September 1966, would "offer associate degree curricula, the third and fourth years of baccalaureate programs, postgraduate work, and research." The resolutions were adopted by the Executive Committee and, on January 8, 1966, by the Board of Trustees. The Capitol campus of the Pennsylvania State University had been formally established.

Walker has stated (1968) that by November 14, 1965, when the governor formally requested that the university develop the Olmsted complex, the basic decisions regarding purpose and structure had already been made and agreed to by Walker, Scranton, Roger W. Rowland, chairman of the Penn State Board of Trustees, and Clifton Jones, secretary of commerce for Pennsylvania, who was involved in the attempt to secure employment for the 11,000 persons who would be idled when the Air Force base was closed. Approval was secured from the Executive Committee of the board even before the first curriculum had been developed for the new campus; the first staff discussions to develop a list of curricula which might be offered in the liberal arts area did not take place until December 1965. Even as late as February 25, 1966 —when formal application was made to the Department of Health, Education and Welfare to secure the Olmsted facilities for Penn State—no decisions had been made as to what programs would be offered or what courses these programs would contain.

On February 23, 1966, Walker sent a letter to Otis C. McCreary (1966b), chairman of the State Board of Education, "requesting your approval [of the new institution] before we make a formal announcement calling for student applications," although the accompanying memorandum to the board (1966c) itself called only for "the concurrence of the State Board of Education." Walker's memo repeated the arguments presented earlier for the development of an upper division institution and did not outline those areas in which instruction would be offered; it did, however, project the initial 1966 enrollment at between 250 and 400 students. Walker also informed the board that the Susquehanna Valley Graduate Center would be moved to the new campus and would "become part of the graduate division of the Capitol Campus." The board (1966, p. 30-4) approved a resolution that Penn State "be authorized to proceed with the development of the Capitol Campus" at its March 10, 1966, meeting, and the last possible legal hurdle had been cleared.

Planning continued up to and through the opening of the Capitol campus—with eighteen students—in September 1966. According to Walker (1968), the institution was not really opened until September 1967, when the first full class was admitted; it was necessary, however, to have some students in the buildings from the beginning. Thus, fourteen months after the governor's first approach to Walker, the first students—transfers from the University Park campus and from other commonwealth campuses—were enrolled to begin work toward as yet undefined bachelor's degrees in humanities and social sciences. Students also attended selected associate degree programs which, according to Coleman Herpel (1965), Capitol campus director, were not in any way considered the first two years of the offerings of the Capitol campus but antedated the campus and were administered, for two years, by the director.

Thus, the eighth upper division institution began operation, first with eighteen students and, a year later, with over 320 students. By 1967, the first curricula, including liberal arts, engineering, business, and bachelor of technology courses, had been instituted, and the associate degree programs had been phased out. Local community college supporters were still not completely assured;[2] the establishment of the Capitol campus had obviously been a pragmatic response to a fluid situation, and situations had been known to change. For the moment, however, Capitol campus remained an upper division institution, the third to open in 1966 and the ninth (including the revamped New School College) to open within the decade 1956–1966.

[2] Although community college supporters were probably not aware of its existence, a letter from Walker to Frank Hawkins (1966a), a member of the Council of Higher Education, on March 19, 1966, stated that "inevitably this [enrollment of freshmen and sophomores] will become necessary sometime in the future. Students with different orientation, outlook, motivation, and ability are going to be attracted to the University programs who will not be applicants for admission to the Community College."

Eight

Conclusions and Conjecture

Between 1655—when Harvard College expanded its baccalaureate offerings from three to four years, thus creating the "traditional" American pattern—and the Second World War, attempts to modify the organizational structure of the baccalaureate program were usually related to one of two major movements in American higher education: to provide a measure of acceleration through a general shortening of the baccalaureate degree or to separate preparatory from university work within the college course. The latter movement led to the development of early junior colleges as two-year

157

institutions tied to the secondary education system and also contributed to the establishment of the first upper division institutions, baccalaureate-granting colleges which require completion of two years of college work for admission and which begin their own offerings at the junior year. Upper division institutions established following the Second World War also reflected the earlier concern for separation of preparatory and university work, at least to the extent that they built upon the work of junior colleges, themselves an outgrowth of this concern. More important, later upper division institutions reflected changing social, industrial, and educational factors; with the rapidly expanding needs for baccalaureate education in the 1950's and 1960's, upper division institution appeared to develop as a logical conclusion to the existing system of publicly supported education.

As early as the 1850's, Henry Tappan of the University of Michigan decided that the work of the American college was secondary, or preparatory, in nature; basing his conclusions on the German model of gymnasium and university, he deduced that American colleges (or universities, as they were sometimes called) were not offering truly advanced, or university-level, work. Unlike his later supporters, such as W. W. Folwell at Minnesota, William Rainey Harper at Chicago, and David Starr Jordan and Ray Lyman Wilbur at Stanford, Tappan did not propose separating the two functions. Rather, having recognized that two functions existed, Tappan moved to "perfect" the gymnasial function within the university itself.

Another distinction between Tappan and those who later advocated the bisection of the American college and the relegation of its component parts to either the high school or the university grew out of Tappan's equation of the entire college, as it then existed, with preparatory work. To Tappan, bisection of the college was not an issue, for there was nothing to bisect. Later educators, particularly Folwell and Harper, felt that the university should rid itself of its nonuniversity functions. Harper's opinion, coupled with the determination that the logical breaking point between secondary and university work came after the second year in the existing college structure, was a primary factor in the early decisions not only to establish independent junior colleges but to tie these new "colleges" to institutions of secondary education, the American high schools.

By the early twentieth century, several junior colleges had been established as two-year general education programs, comparable to the first two years of college study but administratively and theoretically linked to the secondary school. During the 1920's, four-year junior colleges were developed, tying the thirteenth and fourteenth years of education more firmly to the rest of preparatory education through a reorganization of the "middle" and secondary schools. Although this form of organization never gained support outside a few communities, primarily in California, it emphasized the place of the early junior college as a nonuniversity institution and directly influenced the decisions to establish several of the first upper division institutions in this country.

As early as 1861, the University of Georgia (then Franklin College) had reorganized its program to separate the first two years (the College Institute) from the last (the College Proper) and to tie the institute to the secondary department. This decision—an ineresting but isolated precursor of later developments—was primarily a result of local political and financial considerations; any chances for continuing success which the experiment may have had were abruptly ended by the Civil War. By 1935, when the College of the Pacific abolished its own lower division and relegated its freshman and sophomore years to a newly created public junior college, the example of the University of Georgia had long been forgotten. At Pacific, the reasons for choosing the upper division form of organization were predicated on the president's beliefs regarding the proper distinction between preparatory (lower division) and university (upper division) work—themselves based to a great extent on the thinking of Jordan and Alexis Lange in California—and on the financial difficulties of the institution in the depths of the depression. President Tully Knoles believed that his organizational reform was based in sound educational theory. To Knoles, as to Harper and to Robert Maynard Hutchins at the University of Chicago, the distinction between the sophomore and junior years of the American college was at least equally as important as the distinction between the end of baccalaureate study and the beginning of graduate work. This conviction, which also led to a series of organizational reforms at Chicago in 1931 and 1933—the result of which was creation of a four-year high school-college unit and a number of two-year university units—was a direct outgrowth of the earlier statements of Tappan, Folwell, Jordan, and Wilbur.

To a great extent, these early reformers were correct in their analysis of the dual function which the American college was performing, although they apparently failed to accept the reasons for this development and the distinctions from the German model on which they based their thinking. The American college did combine elements of the German gymnasium and university in its curricular offerings, in large measure because of the historical development of the high school in this country as a constantly expanding unit between existing, but fluctuating, elementary and collegiate instructional programs. Those who, in the late nineteenth century, imported the German method of instruction—without which the American university would never have developed—failed to distinguish between the methodology which they admired and the organization in which it had been originally housed, an organization which had no counterpart in the existing American system. Most early attempts to create upper division institutions in the United States may be seen, in part, as attempts to introduce a measure of German structure into institutions which had earlier adopted the German methodology.

The direct influence of the German model was most clearly evident in the establishment of Concordia Senior College and the New School College. The educational system of the Lutheran Church—Missouri Synod, of which Concordia is a part, was directly modeled on the German system, even to the extent of calling the constituent institutions gymnasia rather than colleges. There had been no structural changes in this system, which included ten preparatory institutions (through grade fourteen) and a seminary (for "graduate" work), from its inception in 1839 to the creation of the senior college after the Second World War; the decision to create an additional institution to offer the baccalaureate degree and the work of the traditional junior and senior collegiate years in Ameriican institutions was a direct outgrowth of a desire to accommodate the synod system to the prevailing form of American education. Because the German model on which the old synod system was based already provided for the equivalent of high schools, junior colleges, and universities, the only remaining need was for the upper division of the American college. Folwell and Harper would have been pleased to see the creation of a collegiate institution, such as Concordia, which recognized the gymnasial function of the first two years and built upon it, while retaining its own university level and preparing for graduate education.

The New School Senior College, like the upper division institution at the College of the Pacific, was a result of both practical (passage of the G.I. bill) and educational considerations. A vast majority of the graduate faculty at the New School—the only unit within the school authorized to give degrees—was European in background; the New School itself, in its noncredit offerings, traditionally had been oriented toward adult education. Given Dean Hans Simons' desire to provide an underpinning to the graduate programs and to bring the graduate faculty into greater contact with undergraduate students and given the emphasis on education for adults and the background of the faculty, the creation of an institution to serve older students in the university segment of a baccalaureate program was logical. Although the timing might have been different without the impetus of the G.I. bill, which provided a potential adult student body at no cost to either the student or the institution, the concepts on which it was based would eventually have led to creation of an upper division institution at the New School.

The last major educational reform based on the theory of the bisected college was the 1942 decision to "relocate" the baccalaureate degree at the University of Chicago, a decision which defined the baccalaureate as signifying the conclusion of general education and placed that conclusion at the end of the traditional sophomore year. Following the Second World War, the rapid expansion of junior colleges made discussion of the appropriate point at which to break the baccalaureate degree unnecessary; furthermore, the changing demands of society for education and the changing needs of industry led to the large-scale introduction of vocational or semiprofessional offerings in the junior colleges, which no longer saw themselves as providing only the first half of the baccalaureate degree.

Moreover, following the Second World War, many educators turned their attention away from possible structural reforms to more necessary reforms in the content and the availability of American higher education. Although modification of the "traditional" pattern of two-year or four-year institutions of higher education might not have been the optimal means of achieving greater equality of opportunity for higher education in the 1950's and 1960's, such modification was considered with surprising rarity. In most instances, an "innovative" pattern involved adding another unit within the existing structural pattern rather than reexamining the relevance or effectiveness of that pattern, which, in many ways, was the outgrowth of the reexaminations of earlier years.

Beginning with the creation of Flint College in 1956, educators found themselves faced with one of two situations, each of which might lead to development of a new upper division institution. On the one hand, the number of junior college graduates might create a need for additional baccalaureate programs, while the existence of the junior colleges precluded providing the freshman and sophomore years. On the other hand, the need for specific baccalaureate education (such as engineering at Dearborn) might be determined, with local junior colleges once again obviating the necessity of creating a full four-year institution.

In either case, the existence of large numbers of junior colleges led educators to consider the feasibility of establishing institutions which would begin where the junior colleges left off. Thus, at Florida Atlantic University, Flint College, the University of West Florida, Richmond College, and the Dearborn campus, a need for some baccalaureate offerings was determined; the existence of a local junior college—and the decision not to convert that institution to four-year status—led planners to establish upper division institutions in each case. Although the local political, economic, and social forces differed, causing differing patterns of development in terms of the duration and the direction of the discussions preceding establishment, each of these institutions was similar to the others in terms of the underlying assumptions: baccalaureate need and junior college existence.

Yet, particularly where decisions were based primarily on stated industrial needs, such as at the Dearborn campus of the University of Michigan, significant enrollment problems have arisen. The creation of the Dearborn campus between August 1955 and November 1956 was the direct result of negotiations initiated by the Ford Motor Company in response to a decision that a minimum of 1,150 college graduates annually would be needed to meet the manpower requirements. As the Dearborn Campus Planning Study Committee of the University of Michigan (1969, p. i) stated, "The Ford Motor Company invited The University to place a branch campus at this location and recommended that The University secure adequate operating funds to provide for an enrollment of 2,800 students to help alleviate shortages of professional manpower in the area. The University responded by establishing an upper division campus."

Following a review of the Dearborn enrollment (from thirty-four students in 1959 to a maximum of 777 in the fall of 1968), the committee—which was charged (p. 1) "to evaluate the experience since 1956 and to chart the academic objectives, directions of development, and administrative structure" for the future—concluded that (p. 10) "it seems unlikely that substantial enrollment increases will result at Dearborn in the immediate future by the community college route." Noting also that the (successful) attempt to maintain admissions standards comparable to those at Ann Arbor had limited the potential to draw on community or junior college graduates, the committee recommended (pp. 33, 34) that "the Campus continue to maintain high graduation standards while adopting flexible admission standards that will permit it to serve a more diverse group of high school graduates"; more basic, however, was the recommendation that "lower division programming should be initiated in the Fall of 1970."

Unlike events surrounding the establishment and modification of Flint College, in which community sentiment played a significant role, the events surrounding the establishment and (proposed) modification of the Dearborn campus are more directly related to early failures to look beyond the stated needs of industry and the availability of both land and financial support for construction. The initial decisions to establish a branch at Dearborn had been based on the potential for enrollment from the students' standpoint; moreover, unlike the situation at those other upper division institutions in which no attempt was made to survey potential student interest, decisions at Dearborn were predicated on anticipated demands for graduates as opposed to anticipated demand for baccalaureate education based on demographic and other data.

Admittedly, the factors surrounding the failure to reach one-third of projected enrollment during a decade of operation are more complex than may be implied above. Admissions standards—coupled with the proximity of the Ann Arbor campus as a competing institution—surely affected the Dearborn drawing power, as did the decision to concentrate on cooperative educational programs, requested by industry but perhaps inappropriate for the vocational desires of a community college student. Finally, although not directly related to enrollment difficulties, the inability to establish graduate programs at the Dearborn campus despite the original plans, severely limited the ability to develop or maintain a faculty identified with and committed to the Dearborn campus.

The Dearborn planners were not, however, faced with one decision which other planners both faced and met, that of conversion—or lack of conversion—of two-year institutions to four-year institutions as an alternative to establishment of a separate upper division college. In the majority of cases, the initial determination of need for baccalaureate-level education was followed by the decision—suggested if not made by some statewide agency—not to convert a local junior college. This pattern is consistent with that suggested by Richard Gott (1968, p. 63) in those states in which a central agency did not have the authority to resist "local areas [which] tend to take the initiative in promoting four-year colleges when the need becomes great enough and consider an established two-year college as the logical basis for a four-year college."

Gott also concludes that "when statewide planning fails to provide four-year college facilities in a given area of proven need,

the two-year college will encounter irreconcilable problems in insti-
tutionalizing itself as a two-year college"; thus, strong support for
conversion came from within local junior colleges at Pensacola,
Richmond, and, for a time, Flint. The eventual decision not to
allow conversion was based more on a concern for the eventual loss
of a structural form and its services than on any evidence of the
inability of a four-year structure to offer both associate (two-year
terminal or transfer) and baccalaureate degrees, as is being done
at several large universities, those institutions studied by Gott, and
eight of nine recently converted junior colleges surveyed by the
author.

Pratt Senior College and the Capitol campus of the Pennsylvania State University offer slightly differing patterns, although
each of these institutions was also based upon the assumption that
other institutions could and would offer the first two years of the
baccalaureate program. At Pratt Institute, these years would be
offered by the institute itself; the senior college was merely an administrative convenience to enable the institute to offer liberal arts
degrees to its own dissatisfied professional students. At Penn State,
the decision to create an upper division institution—as opposed to a
four-year program—was based upon the existence of other institutions which were already offering the first two years, although the
more basic decision to establish a new institution was the result of
the availability of land and facilities more than of any felt need to
increase the overall educational offerings of the area.

Political considerations played a significantly greater role in
the establishment of upper division colleges after 1956, in part because all those institutions established before that date were private
and all but one (Pratt) established after 1956 were public. The
distinction between public and private is also related to the distinction between the earlier and the later reasons for creation of upper
division institutions; the later, public institutions were much more
responsive than the private institutions to the growing numbers of
junior colleges (which were predominantly public in these areas)
and of their graduates, as well as to pressures from local industries
or politicians for an institution to serve the specific needs of their
area. Furthermore, public institutions were affected to a much

greater degree by the availability of land or facilities. Capitol campus was begun for this reason, several other institutions were established on the condition of available land or assistance with facilities construction, and the University of West Florida was not established in the late 1950's in large part because of the sudden unavailability of a naval base.

Although the need for legislative approval or funding or both affected the development of public institutions, legislative involvement played little or no part in the decision to establish an upper division institution per se; legislative concern was focused primarily upon the decision to establish any institution at a given time or place. In Florida, legislative pressure to create some institution led planners to develop an upper division institution in Pensacola for lack of another feasible alternative, while in Michigan, legislative and State Board of Education review almost prevented the conversion of Flint College from an upper division to a four-year institution in 1964–1965.

Four colleges have been significantly modified as a response to changing conditions since their establishment as upper division institutions, assuming successful implementation of the recommendations of the Dearborn Study Committee. At College of the Pacific, enrollment problems (although only perceived as potential problems), problems of accreditation, and severe problems in terms of the necessary cooperative arrangements with the local junior college all contributed to the decision to return to a four-year status. At the New School the existing senior college was phased out and a new upper division college, more responsive to the needs of both the institution and its students in the 1960's, was created. Finally, in Michigan, the apparent inability of the upper division institutions to draw students at the junior year both made the University of Michigan amenable to the Flint community desires for a four-year institution and led the university to reconsider the status of its Dearborn campus.

In looking to the future, one must be aware of some of the operational difficulties which existing upper division institutions have encountered. Three of these institutions—Flint College, the Dearborn campus, and Florida Atlantic University—have made significant attempts over a minimum of five years to reach substantial enrollment levels; other institutions, such as Richmond College, the Capitol campus, and the University of West Florida have not been in operation long enough to give any indication of whether their long-term enrollment projections will be met. Concordia College, Pratt Senior College, and the New School College have never set large enrollment goals, while the situation at the College of the Pacific was somewhat abnormal not only because of its unique relationship with the public junior college but because of the years—depression and post-World War Two—during which it operated.

Each of the institutions which set significant long-term enrollment projections and which has been in operation for a minimum of five years has failed to meet its projections from the outset; in the two Michigan institutions, this failure has contributed to the eventual recommendation that freshman and sophomore classes be added. Florida Atlantic University anticipated an enrollment of approximately 4,900 students in the fall of 1969 as opposed to the original estimates that F.A.U. would enroll 4,000 students by its second year of operation and 10,000 students by 1970. (Yet, despite this experience, Florida International University, to be located in Miami less than sixty miles from Florida Atlantic, is projected to enroll 4,000 students at its opening in 1972, 10,000 students by 1975, and 20,000 by 1980.)

Although the reasons for this failure differ from institution to institution, a major problem in each case has been the inability to assume the constant and direct flow of students from the sophomore to the junior years as occurs in a four-year college situation. Moreover, each of these institutions was competing for its students without adequate dormitory facilities and without many of the extracurricular activities, such as big-time football, which other public institutions could offer. Thus, the institutions suffered not only from their newness and lack of reputation and from their peculiar role as upper division institutions but also from a relative disadvantage when compared with those institutions with which they were competing for the junior college transfer. Both the University of West Florida and the Capitol campus appear to have adequate dormitory facilities—in terms of a percentage of their total projected enrollment—and Richmond College, without dormitories at present, is a unit of an educational system, the City University of New York, in which no institution has either dormitories or big-time football.

Another reason for the failure of these institutions to meet their projected enrollment goals may be found within the goals themselves, which often appear to have been based either on rough guesses or on untested assumptions as to the percentage of junior college graduates who continue their education and would wish to do so at an upper division institution. Florida Atlantic, for example, has never attained the goals which were set for it; yet, the number of students presently enrolled at Florida Atlantic is approximately equal to the number in the upper division at either Florida State University or the University of Florida.

Moreover, upper division institutions may face unique difficulties in the distribution of majors which their students choose; conversely, failure to emphasize appropriate majors during recruitment may hinder attempts to meet enrollment projections. Specifically, Florida Atlantic has discovered that its students' choices of majors differ significantly from students' choices at four-year state institutions in that Florida Atlantic students are more heavily oriented toward teaching and business programs and less oriented toward "pure" liberal arts. One possible explanation is that junior college students—who compose the bulk of the Florida Altantic and of most upper division institution student bodies—have significantly different career goals or expectations from those of students entering four-year institutions and are more inclined to choose major fields which lead to immediate reward or employment as opposed to those which lead to continued study at a graduate institution.

Most upper division institutions have also encountered difficulty because of their inability to offer lower division courses which are often needed as prerequisites for further study or are desired simply as general education options during a student's normal upper division studies. To a great extent, this difficulty is less real than perceived, as there is no reason why an upper division institution cannot offer certain lower division courses; in fact, some programs such as language, music, and other fine arts do not lend themselves to the preparatory-professional dichotomy on which the upper division institution is predicated but require a parallel availability of both general and specialized courses throughout the four years of collegiate study.

Perhaps the greatest danger to those upper division institutions now in operation lies within the concern over enrollment. Admittedly, most upper division institutions have failed to meet the initial enrollment projections; this failure, however, may be due to any number of factors, of which "upper divisionness" is only one. As at Flint and Dearborn the danger always exists that those responsible for planning will not look beyond the obvious structural form of their institution in attempting to discern the reasons for inadequate enrollment. A decision to add freshman and sophomore classes will obviously add students; it may even increase the effective utilization of faculty (who otherwise have no lower division courses to teach in addition to their specialty) or may increase the number of "draw-through" students who continue directly into the junior year. Nonetheless, the enrollment figures at Flint College since its expansion to a four-year institution do not indicate that conversion, in itself, can solve many of the problems which led initially to low enrollments. And, at Dearborn, no change in structure —unless accompanied by a change in the admissions policy which prevents the campus from serving the Detroit metropolitan area— will lead to a significant upswing in enrollment.

Concrete steps can be taken—both in those institutions already in operation and in those planned for the future—to reduce the probability of inadequate enrollments. Perhaps most basic is a reevaluation of the assumptions concerning junior college graduates who will continue their education; use of overly optimistic figures can lead only to difficulties at the upper division institution. Faculty exchange programs—which allow the upper division faculty to teach at other institutions, primarily local junior colleges—can also be of use, not only to increase effective faculty utilization but also to improve the drawing power of the upper division institution among junior college students who may be attracted to the institution or to a given major by a particularly rewarding experience under a visiting professor.

Furthermore, cooperative arrangements between upper division institutions and junior colleges, which provide the lifeline for the former, can always be improved. Upper division institutions cannot be expected to develop their curricula to build upon the offerings of a half dozen junior colleges; yet, increased communications, improved counseling at the junior college in cooperation with senior college counselors, and a willingness on the part of the upper division institution to consciously seek out junior college graduates and provide programs suited to their needs will provide both short-term and long-term benefits. Counseling and recruitment may draw increasing numbers of students to the upper division institution; over the long run, however, the ability to provide satisfying and rewarding educational opportunities for the junior college graduates who have attended will determine the success of later recruiting efforts.

Future upper division institutions will probably place less emphasis than before on the liberal arts degree and increasingly greater emphasis on the newly developing Bachelor of Technology degree or its equivalent. Just as early junior colleges shifted their emphasis from exclusively prebaccalaureate to vocational and semiprofessional offerings, upper division institutions must respond to the growing needs for professional and vocational baccalaureate degrees. This statement does not imply that upper division institutions will or should abandon their liberal arts offerings; yet, to the extent that assumptions concerning junior college graduates' interests and the future needs of society are correct, upper division institutions should move to meet their needs. As public institutions, with unique opportunities for close and effective cooperation with public junior colleges, upper division institutions appear to be one vehicle for offering the newly developing professionally oriented baccalaureate degree, thus both serving society and increasing their own drawing power with junior college students.

Yet, despite stated fears that converted junior colleges (or any four-year institution, for that matter) will leave only second-class two-year vocational or technical programs, the bisected baccalaureate program may not be the only vehicle for providing both the functions of the "traditional" junior, or community, college and the newly developing professionally oriented baccalaureate degrees. The John Jay College of Criminal Justice of the City University of New York has successfully offered both two-year terminal and transfer degrees and four-year baccalaureate programs for five years without the apparent atrophy of the two-year programs; more recently, a four-year experimental professional college—to combine terminal and transfer two-year programs with professionally oriented baccalaureate programs—has been approved by the Board of Higher Education in New York City. And, as reported by Donald Janes (1969), several hundred four-year colleges and universities throughout the country presently offer some form of subbaccalaureate programs including two-year associate degrees.

Obviously, the above discussion is predicated on the assumption that future upper division institutions will be predominantly public, rather than private, colleges and universities. To date, only three private upper division institutions have been created which offer liberal arts programs, although a number of specialty institutions—including Otis Art Institute of Los Angeles, Pacific Oaks College (elementary education) of Los Angeles, and Walsh College of Accountancy and Business Administration of Detroit—have been developed as or converted to upper division institutions in order to draw upon the increasing number of junior college graduates. Upper division institutions, as they have developed since the Second World War, are most often a capstone to a public system of education; they provide for the junior college graduate an outlet no longer available in overcrowded four-year public institutions. And the trend toward public upper division institutions will probably not change in the foreseeable future.

Predicated upon assumptions of societal need—whether demonstrated or assumed by power groups which can affect public policy—upper division institutions are a logical response for a public system facing enrollment pressures at the junior year or a need for additional baccalaureate education. If junior colleges did not exist, if they were not predominantly public, or if the hesitancy to convert or expand them did not exist, upper division colleges would not develop in increasing numbers and locations. Yet, public junior colleges are the fastest growing segment of American higher education; there is every indication that public upper division institutions will be developed apace.

Moreover, the public upper division institution will be predominantly an urban institution. Historically, state-supported public institutions have been located away from the major (present) urban areas; yet, the establishment of public junior colleges in urban areas has created a growing and unmet need for publicly supported baccalaureate-level education. Richmond College is located in New York City; in theory, Florida Atlantic University served the Miami metropolitan area. Upper division institutions presently in various stages of development throughout the country are almost exclusively planned for urban centers: Illinois is developing upper division institutions for Springfield and Chicago; Minnesota is considering an upper division institution in Minneapolis-St. Paul; the state of Washington has begun legislative hearings on the possible development of an upper division institution in Seattle; the Florida Board of Control has approved new upper division institutions for Miami and Jacksonville; and the Texas legislature, in approving plans for three of six new baccalaureate-granting institutions recommended by the State Coordinating Council, indicated that two of these (located in Dallas and the Midland-Odessa area) will be upper division institutions.

The establishment of upper division institutions in urban areas not only meets a growing need but also gives some assurance of less difficulty in meeting enrollment goals since graduates of junior colleges can reasonably be expected to travel to the new institutions. The alternative, as suggested in the Texas proposal for an upper division institution in the Midland-Odessa area and in the recently approved proposal for establishment of an upper division unit of the State University of New York in the Rome-Herkimer-Utica area, is development of upper division institutions as regional institutions to serve a number of junior colleges. Regional upper division institutions, if developed, may face enrollment problems similar to those presently in operation, although adequate dormitory facilities and an active campaign to secure both students and public acceptance can make them a logical answer to the upper division needs of less heavily settled areas with expanding systems of junior colleges.

Existing upper division institutions—public as well as private—tend to offer some postbaccalaureate studies, although the existing pattern makes projection to the future difficult. In all except the Dearborn campus, where the institution is public, planners have envisioned at least master's programs, while several have anticipated offering doctorates. In some cases, such as Richmond College of the City University of New York, doctoral work is not a reasonable alternative since all doctoral work is offered centrally by a university graduate center. In other cases, such as the two Florida institutions, a struggle has developed between the upper division institutions and the established state universities, the former desiring the right to offer doctorates (for both educational and prestige reasons)' and the latter claiming (with some degree of correctness)' that the limited resources for doctoral programs should not be fragmented among institutions which do not now have the necessary expertise or facilities. The Dearborn experience, however, suggests that without a minimum of master's degree offerings, an institution may encounter difficulty in recruiting both faculty and students.

Future upper division institutions—such as those proposed for Miami, Jacksonville, Dallas, Houston, Minneapolis, and Chicago—will probably offer work through the master's degree, although this decision appears more dependent on need and availability of resources at existing institutions than on any determination that the master's degree is more closely tied to the bachelor's degree than to doctoral studies. Whether the new institutions will eventually offer doctoral programs depends on the availability of resources within the system of which they are a part and on the political strength which the new institutions can muster on their own behalf.

Future development of upper division institutions may be expected, especially in those areas where a system of community or junior colleges is nearing completion; the only mitigating factor would appear to be large-scale failures among those upper division institutions now in operation. Although many existing upper division institutions are facing problems, both real and perceived, the structure of these institutions (save the Dearborn campus) will probably not be modified in the near future.

Moreover, many of the problems which the existing colleges presently face can be avoided by newly developed upper division institutions. Given an awareness of the potential difficulty in securing adequate enrollment—and of the reasons for this difficulty— as well as an awareness of related problems of faculty recruitment and utilization without adequate graduate-level programs, upper division institutions can set realistic guidelines to ensure "successful" operation. Admittedly, the "should" of future development may not correspond with the "will" of actual planning and operation any more than it has in the past. Although not untypical of that in American higher education, planning for existing upper division institutions has been characterized by a distinct paucity of investigation into the strengths and weaknesses of those institutions which have faced similar problems because of their unique organizational structure.

The conclusion appears unescapable that additional upper division institutions will be developed during the next two decades if for no other reason than that this alternative appears to be the most viable in relation to either conversion of existing junior colleges or creation of many four-year institutions which would then have to provide space both for their own sophomores and for graduates of junior colleges. This statement, however, assumes a growing demand for baccalaureate education, a demand which both builds upon and feeds the growing numbers of junior colleges. To the extent that this assumption is correct, it raises several questions which may (or should) affect the future development of upper division institutions.

Ideally, institutional structure is a function of the educational needs which the institution must serve; in fact, however, institutional structure in the United States has become a given within the framework of a two-year or four-year degree. Thus, upper division institutions have developed since World War Two as two-year programs, a structure dictated more by the existence of both two-year (associate) and four-year (baccalaureate) programs than by consideration of the educational needs. Similarly, conversion of junior colleges has been rejected in each system in which it has been considered because of the fear that junior colleges would cease to be two-year institutions and would thus cease to perform many of the worthwhile functions which they, as opposed to four-year institutions, now do.

The dichotomy of structure and function, however, need not exist. Four-year institutions can offer and have offered extensive community service and extension programs; four-year institutions also can offer and have offered associate degree or two-year curricula, either as part of their normal four-year progression or as separate divisions within a larger institution. To the extent that four-year institutions—offering both associate and baccalaureate work—are viable, there is no reason to continue the development of upper division institutions. Moreover, if demand for both two- and four-year educational programs continues to grow, the possibility of large-scale conversion of both junior and upper division colleges to four-year institutions may arise as the most financially and educationally sound alternative.

In any case, the way in which future upper division institutions develop will greatly affect the development of existing junior colleges. If upper division institutions expand their offerings in non-liberal arts areas as suggested above, the status and desirability of present "career" or "terminal" junior college programs will be greatly increased, in turn increasing the enrollments within these programs during the first two collegiate years. If, on the other hand, upper division institutions choose to concentrate on liberal arts programs to the exclusion of other forms of baccalaureate education, they run the risk of failing not only to serve growing societal needs but also to draw sufficient enrollment to ensure continued efficient operation.

Existing upper division institutions have demonstrated that this institution is workable, despite operational problems; given an unwillingness to convert existing junior colleges or to offer associate and baccalaureate degrees within one institution, upper division institutions will continue to increase as the capstone to growing numbers of public educational systems. With a nonexistent system of public education beyond high school, the junior college, upper division college, and four-year institution would not be the ideal structure to develop; however, with the existing structural bases in American higher education, it is the most likely both to develop and to succeed.

References

Unpublished documents, with the exception of letters to the author and transcripts of interviews on file with the author, are located at the campus (or parent institution) of the institution to which they are related.

Academy for Educational Development, Inc. "Elements of a Master Plan for Higher Education in Pennsylvania: A Report to the State Board of Education of the Commonwealth of Pennsylvania." 1965.

ADAMS, C. K. *Annual Report of the President of Cornell University*. Ithaca, N.Y.: Cornell University, 1890.

Administrative Committee on Long-Range Development. "Penn State's Future . . . The Job and a Way to Do It." 1965.

177

ANGELL, J. B. *The President's Report to the Board of Regents.* Ann Arbor, Mich.: University of Michigan, 1890.

ASHLER, P. F. Interview at Tallahassee, Fla. November 22, 1968.

AUSTILL, A. "A New Senior College." Memo to J. R. Everett, September 8, 1965. (On file at the New School, New York, N.Y.)

AUSTILL, A. Interview at New York, N.Y. December 12, 1968.

BARNARD, F. A. P. *Annual Report of the President of Columbia College for the Year 1885–86.* New York: Columbia University, 1886.

BASKIN, S. (Ed.) *Higher Education: Some Newer Developments.* New York: McGraw-Hill, 1965.

BATES, G. J. "The Future of Higher Education in the Flint Area." Report of the Joint Committee to Study the Needs for Higher Education in the Flint Area. 1964. (On file at Flint College, Flint, Mich.)

BECKER, J. "Using Computers in a New University Library." *American Library Association Bulletin,* 1965, *59,* 823–826.

BLOCH, C. D. "Education in Our Community: A History of the Public Schools of Stockton, California." Unpublished Master's thesis, University of the Pacific, 1962.

BLOOM, B. S., and WARD, F. C. "The Chicago Bachelor of Arts Degree After Ten Years." *The Journal of Higher Education,* 1952, *23,* 459–476.

Board of Higher Education of New York City. *A Long-Range Plan for the City University of New York. Report of the Board of Higher Education Committee to Look to the Future.* New York, 1962.

Board of Higher Education of New York City. *Proceedings of the Board of Higher Education of The City of New York: 1962.* New York, 1963.

Board of Higher Education of New York City. *Master Plan for The City University of New York* (with November 1964 Amendments: College of Police Science and Hunter Collge School of Social Work). New York, 1964. (a)

Board of Higher Education of New York City. *Proceedings of the Board of Higher Education of The City of New York: 1963.* New York, 1964. (b)

Board of Higher Education of New York City. "A Report of the Committee of the Board of Higher Education to Determine the Possible Need for a Four-Year Tax-Supported College in the Borough of Richmond as a Unit of The City University of New York." 1964. (c)

Board of Higher Education of New York City. *Proceedings of the Board of Higher Education of The City of New York: 1964.* New York, 1965. (a)

Board of Higher Education of New York City. "A Recommendation on Implementation of the Board of Higher Education Resolution That The City of New York Establish a Four-Year College in the Borough of Richmond as a Unit of The City University of New York." 1965. (b)

Board of Higher Education of New York City. "Upper Division (Third and Fourth Year) College: A Recommendation on Implementation of the Board of Higher Education Resolution That The City of New York Establish a Four-Year College in the Borough of Richmond as a Unit of The City University of New York." 1965. (c)

Board of Higher Education of New York City. *Proceedings of the Board of Higher Education of The City of New York: 1965.* New York, 1966.

Board of Higher Education of New York City. *Proceedings of the Board of Higher Education of The City of New York: 1966.* New York, 1967.

BOUCHER, C. S. *The Chicago College Plan.* Chicago: University of Chicago Press, 1935.

BRICK, M. *Forum and Focus for the Junior College Movement.* New York: Bureau of Publications, Teachers College, Columbia University, 1964.

BRONSON, W. C. *History of Brown University 1764–1914.* Providence, R.I.: Brown University, 1914.

BROOKS, R. P. *The University of Georgia Under Sixteen Administrations, 1785–1955.* Athens, Ga.: University of Georgia Press, 1956.

BROWN, S. J. "Present Development of the Secondary Schools According to the Proposed Plan." *The School Review,* 1908, *13*, 15–18.

BRUMBAUGH, A. J. "Report of the Planning Commission for a New University at Boca Raton." 1961.

BRUMBAUGH, A. J. Letter to Robert A. Altman, December 4, 1968.

BRUMBAUGH, A. J., *and* BLEE, M. R. *Higher Education and Florida's Future. Vol. 1. Recommendations and General Staff Report.* Gainesville, Fla.: University of Florida Press, 1956.

BURNS, R. E. "President's Report, March 28, 1950." (a) (On file at University of the Pacific, Stockton, Calif.)

BURNS, R. E. "President's Report, October 20, 1950." (b) (On file at University of the Pacific, Stockton, Calif.)

BURNS, R. E. Interview at Stockton, Calif. October 7, 1968.

BUTLER, N. M. *Annual Report of the President to the Trustees*. New York: Columbia University, 1902.

CAMPBELL, W. G. "The Hillsboro Four-Year Junior College." *The Junior College Journal*, 1932, *2*, 263–268.

City University of New York. "Minutes of the Meeting of the Administrative Council, February 25, 1965."

College of the Pacific. *Bulletin of the College of the Pacific: Junior College Issue*. Stockton, Calif., 1934.

College of the Pacific. *Bulletin of the College of the Pacific: General College Issue*. Stockton, Calif., 1935.

College of the Pacific. "Minutes of the Board of Trustees, September 29, 1925–June 15, 1939."

College of the Pacific. *Bulletin of the College of the Pacific. Catalogue Issue 1951; Announcements for 1951–52*. Stockton, Calif., 1951.

College of the Pacific. "Minutes of the Board of Trustees, October 25, 1949–June 18, 1955."

Concordia Senior College. "Self-Survey Report of Concordia Senior College, Fort Wayne, Indiana." 1961.

COOPER, W. J. "Some Advantages Expected to Result from Administering Secondary Education in Two Units of Four Years Each." *The School Review*, 1929, *37*, 335–346.

COULTER, E. M. *College Life in the Old South*. New York: Macmillan, 1928.

COWLEY, W. H. "A Ninety-Year-Old Conflict Erupts Again." *The Educational Record*, 1942, *23*, 192–218.

COWLEY, W. H. "The Three American University Plans." An unpublished, untitled report written for the Fund for the Advancement of Education, 1955.

CULPEPPER, J. B. "Next Steps for Creating the State University at Boca Raton." 1960.

CULPEPPER, J. B. "Summary of Plans for a State University at Boca Raton." 1959 to 1961.

CULPEPPER, J. B. "Report to the Board of Control by the Executive Director for the Biennium July 1, 1962 to June 30, 1964." 1964.

CULPEPPER, J. B. Letter to Robert A. Altman, February 5, 1969.

CULPEPPER, J. B., and TULLY, G. E. "Antecedents to Master Planning for Higher Education in Florida." Florida Board of Regents Staff Study Reports No. 101. 1967.

CUMMINGS, E. Letter to Board of Regents, University of Michigan, December 8, 1954.

CUMMINGS, E. Letter to Marvin L. Niehuss, April 20, 1955.

CUMMINGS, E. Interview at Flint, Mich. April 4, 1968.

DONNELLY, C. Interview at Flint, Mich. April 3, 1968.

EBY, F. "The Four-Year Junior College." *The Junior College Journal,* 1932, *2,* 471–489.

ECKELBERRY, R. H. "Chicago Modifies Its Baccalaureate Program." *Journal of Higher Education,* 1953, *24,* 387–388.

EELLS, W. C. *The Junior College.* Boston: Houghton Mifflin, 1931.

EELLS, W. C. "Abolition of the Lower Division: Early History." *The Junior College Journal,* 1936, *6,* 193–195.

EELLS, W. C. "The Bachelor's Degree—A Junior College Viewpoint." *The Southern Association Quarterly,* 1942, *6,* 355–361. (a)

EELLS, W. C. "The Bachelor's Degree—From the Junior College Standpoint." *The Educational Record,* 1942, *23,* 574–585. (b)

EELLS, W. C., and MARTORANA, S. V. "Curricular Changes in Two-Year Colleges That Become Four-Year Colleges." *Higher Education,* 1957, *13,* 149–153. (a)

EELLS, W. C., and MARTORANA, S. V. "Do Junior Colleges Become Senior Colleges?" *Higher Education,* 1957, *13,* 110–115. (b)

ELIOT, C. W. *President's Report for 1885–86.* Cambridge, Mass.: Harvard University, 1886.

ELIOT, C. W. *President's Report for 1886–87.* Cambridge, Mass.: Harvard University, 1887.

ELIOT, C. W. *President's Report for 1887–88.* Cambridge, Mass.: Harvard University, 1888.

ELIOT, C. W. *President's Report for 1890–91.* Cambridge, Mass.: Harvard University, 1891.

ELIOT, C. W. "The Length of the Baccalaureate Course and Preparation for the Professional Schools." *Journal of Proceedings and Addresses of the National Education Association,* 1903, 496–500.

Evangelical Lutheran Synod of Missouri, Ohio, and Other States. "Report of the Board of Higher Education." In *Proceedings of the Thirty-Ninth Regular Convention of the Evangelical Lutheran Synod of Missouri, Ohio, and Other States, Saginaw, Michigan, June 21–29, 1944.* St. Louis: Concordia, 1944.

Evangelical Lutheran Synod of Missouri, Ohio, and Other States. "Report of the Board for Higher Education." In *Proceedings of the Fortieth Regular Convention of the Evangelical Lutheran Synod of Missouri, Ohio, and Other States Assembled at Chicago, Illinois as the Twenty-Fifth Delegate Synod and as the First Centennial Synod July 20–29, 1947.* St. Louis: Concordia, 1947.

EVERETT, J. R. Interview at New York, N.Y. December 12, 1968.

FARRAND, E. M. *History of the University of Michigan.* Ann Arbor, Mich.: Register, 1885.

FAUST, C. H. "The College at the University of Chicago." *The Southern Association Quarterly,* 1942, *6,* 346–351.

Flint (Michigan) Board of Education. "Suggested Proposal to the University of Michigan in Reply to Their Proposal of May 18." 1952.

Flint (Michigan) Board of Education. "Minutes of the Regular Meeting of April 8, 1964."

Flint (Michigan) Citizen's Committee for the Development of a Four-Year College for Flint. "Summary of Progress Reports 1–5 to the Citizen's Committee for the Development of a Four-Year College for Flint." 1952. (On file at Flint College, Flint, Mich.)

Flint Journal. June 8, 1950 (a); June 11, 1950 (b); November 9, 1962 (a); November 14, 1962 (b); April 9, 1964.

Florida Atlantic University. *Bulletin 1965–66.* Boca Raton, Fla., 1965.

"Florida Master Plans for Record College Enrollment." *American School and University,* 1965, *38,* 28–29.

Florida Times Union (Jacksonville). March 24, 1961.

FOLWELL, W. W. *University Addresses.* Minneapolis: H. W. Wilson, 1909.

Ford Motor Company. "Minutes of Meeting of Administration Committee of the Ford Motor Company, January 11, 1956."

FOWLKES, J. G. "Providing for Education Beyond High School in the Pensacola Area." July 21, 1962. (a)

FOWLKES, J. G. *Providing for Education Beyond High School in the Pensacola Area.* Tallahassee, Fla.: Board of Control, 1962. (b)

FOWLKES, J. G. Telephone interview. January 15, 1969.

FRENCH, D. M. Letter to Willard B. Spaulding, September 26, 1966.

FRENCH, D. M. Interview at Flint, Mich. April 5, 1968.

FRETWELL, E. K., JR. Memo to Albert H. Bowker, November 11, 1964.

FRETWELL, E. K., JR. Letter to Arleigh B. Williamson, January 22, 1965. (a)

FRETWELL, E. K., JR. "A Plan to Establish an Upper-Division College on Staten Island." 1965. (b)

FRETWELL, E. K., JR. Interview at New York, N.Y. February 1, 1968.

GILMAN, D. C. "The Shortening of the College Curriculum." *Educational Record,* 1891, *1,* 1–7.

GOODNOW, F. J. "The Future Policy of the Johns Hopkins University." *School and Society,* 1925, *21,* 618.

GOODSPEED, T. W. *A History of the University of Chicago Founded by John D. Rockefeller: The First Quarter Century.* Chicago: University of Chicago Press, 1916.

GOODSPEED, T. W. *The Story of the University of Chicago, 1890–1925.* Chicago: University of Chicago Press, 1925.

GORMAN, M. Letter to Roscoe O. Bonisteel, November 12, 1954.

GORMAN, M. Memorandum regarding Flint branch of the University of Michigan, n.d.

GOTT, R. H. *Junior College into Four-Year College: Rationale and Result in Two Institutions.* Berkeley, Calif.: Center for Research and Development in Higher Education, 1968.

GUMMERE, R. M. "The Bisected A.B." *The Southern Association Quarterly,* 1942, *6,* 339–345.

HARBESON, J. W. "The Pasadena Junior College Experiment." *The Junior College Journal,* 1931, *2,* 4–10.

HARPER, W. R. *Decennial Report.* Chicago: University of Chicago Press, 1902.

HARPER, W. R. "The Length of the Baccalaureate Course and Preparation for the Professional Schools." *Journal of Proceedings and Addresses of the National Education Association,* 1903, 405–409.

HATCHER, H. A. Letter to Henry Ford II, November 13, 1956.

HEINDEL, R. H. "Inaugural Address, May 5, 1962." (On file at Pratt Institute, Brooklyn, N.Y.)

HEINDEL, R. H. Memo to Education Committee, Board of Trustees, September 28, 1964. (a) (On file at Pratt Institute, Brooklyn, N.Y.)

HEINDEL, R. H. Memo to Louis Sass and Ransom Noble, January 3, 1964. (b)

HEINDEL, R. H. Interview at Middletown, Pa. September 17, 1968.

HENDERSON, A. D. "Memorandum on Flint College Proposal." 1951.

HENDERSON, A. D. Confidential memorandum to the Board of Education, Flint, Michigan, May 20, 1952. (a)

HENDERSON, A. D. Memorandum to Harlan Hatcher, November 18, 1952. (b)

HENDERSON, A. D. Memorandum to Harlan Hatcher, May 6, 1953. (a)

HENDERSON, A. D. "Notes on the Meeting of the Flint College Committee with Members of the Flint Board of Education, January 26, 1953." (b)

HERPEL, C. Interview at Middletown, Pa. September 17, 1968.

HINSDALE, B. A. *History of the University of Michigan.* Ann Arbor, Mich.: University of Michigan, 1906.

HOBSON, F. Letter to Ransom E. Noble, July 9, 1965.

HULL, A. L. *A Historical Sketch of the University of Georgia.* Atlanta: Foote and Davies, 1894.

HUNT, R. D. *History of the College of the Pacific.* Stockton, Calif.: College of the Pacific, 1951.

HUTCHINS, R. M. "The Junior College." *The Educational Record,* 1938, *19,* 5–11.

HUTCHINS, R. M. "The University of Chicago and the Bachelor's Degree." *The Educational Record,* 1942, *23,* 567–573.

HUTCHINS, R. M. *The State of the University 1929–1949.* Chicago: University of Chicago Press, 1949.

IVEY, J. E. "Tentative Plan for a State University at Boca Raton." 1959.

JAMES, E. J. *Education of Business Men: An Address Before the Convention of the American Bankers Association.* New York: W. B. Greene, 1891.

JANES, D. W. "Sub-Baccalaureate Programs in Four-Year Colleges and Universities: Status and Trends." A Report to the American Council on Education, 1969.

JARVIE, L. L. Interview at New York, N.Y. January 11, 1968.

JOHNSON, A. *Pioneer's Progress.* New York: Viking, 1952.

JOHNSON, A. Letter to Hans Simons, February 24, 1958.

JOHNSON, A. Interview at Nyack, N.Y. May 3, 1968.

JORDON, D. S. *Fourth Annual Report of the President of the University.* Trustees Series No. 15. Stanford, Calif.: Stanford University, 1907.

KNOELL, D. M., and MEDSKER, L. L. *From Junior to Senior College: A*

National Study of the Transfer Student. Washington, D.C.: American Council on Education, 1965.

KNOLES, T. C. "President's Report, March 27, 1934." (a) (On file at University of the Pacific, Stockton, Calif.)

KNOLES, T. C. "President's Report, October 23, 1934." (b)

KNOLES, T. C. "President's Report, October, 1935."

KNOLES, T. C. "President's Report, October 27, 1936."

KNOLES, T. C. "President's Report, April 1, 1937."

Laws of Florida: General Laws, 1955. Vol. 1, Pt. 2, Chaps. 29997–30549. Tallahassee, Fla.: State of Florida, 1955.

Laws of Florida: General Laws, 1961. Vol. 1, Pt. 2. Memorials, Resolutions, Chaps. 1–539. Tallahassee, Fla.: State of Florida, 1961.

Laws of Florida: General Laws, 1963. Vol. 1, Pt. 1. Memorials, Resolutions, Chaps. 1–574. Tallahassee, Fla.: State of Florida, 1963.

LEVY, H. L. Memorandum to the City University Administrative Council, April 14, 1964.

LEVY, H. L. Letter to Robert A. Altman, January 20, 1968.

Lutheran Church—Missouri Synod. "Report of the Board for Higher Education." In *Proceedings of the Forty-First Regular Convention of the Lutheran Church—Missouri Synod Assembled at Milwaukee, Wisconsin as the Twenty-Sixth Delegate Synod June 21–30, 1950.* St. Louis: Concordia, 1950.

Lutheran Church—Missouri Synod. "Report of the Board for Higher Education." In *Proceedings of the Forty-Second Regular Convention of the Lutheran Church—Missouri Synod Assembled at Houston, Texas as the Twenty-Seventh Delegate Synod June 17–26, 1953.* St. Louis: Concordia, 1953.

Lutheran Church—Missouri Synod. "Report of the Board for Higher Education." In *Proceedings of the Forty-Third Regular Convention of the Lutheran Church—Missouri Synod Assembled at Saint Paul, Minnesota as the Twenty-Eighth Delegate Synod June 20–29, 1956.* St. Louis: Concordia, 1956.

MCGRATH, E. "The Mission of the New School." 1957.

MARTORANA, S. V. Letter to Robert A. Altman, March 27, 1968.

MERRELL, A. W. Letter to Harlan Hatcher, January 24, 1957.

Middle States Association of Colleges and Universities. "Report of the Evaluation Committee: The New School for Social Research, New York, N.Y. February 14–17, 1960."

MORISON, S. E. *Harvard College in the Seventeenth Century.* Cambridge, Mass.: Harvard University Press, 1936. 2 Vols.

NEEB, M. J. Interview at Fort Wayne, Ind. July 9, 1968. (a)

NEEB, M. J. Letter to Robert A. Altman, August 5, 1968. (b)

New School. *The New School: Courses of Study 1943–44.* New York, 1943.

New School. *The New School Bulletin: School of Politics; School of Philosophy and Liberal Arts.* New York, 1944.

New School. "Minutes, June 22, 1934—February 12, 1945."

New School. "A Self-Study of The New School for Social Research Prepared for Middle States Association of Colleges and Secondary Schools." 1960.

New School. "Report of the Sub-Committee on the B.A. Program." 1964.

New School. "Minutes of the Education Policy Committee, October 1, 1965."

New School. "Minutes of the Education Policy Committee, February 4, 1966."

New York Times. June 22, 1965.

NIEHUSS, M. Letter to Committee on Ways and Means, House of Representatives, Lansing, Mich., April 4, 1955. (a)

NIEHUSS, M. Letter to Everett A. Cummings, April 22, 1955. (b)

NIEHUSS, M. Interview at Ann Arbor, Mich. July 1, 1968.

NOBLE, R. Interview at Brooklyn, N.Y. March 5, 1968.

NOBLE, R. Letter to Robert A. Altman, February 6, 1969.

NOBLE, R., and SASS, L. D. "Proposal for a 'Pratt Senior College.' " 1964. (a)

NOBLE, R., and SASS, L. D. "Proposal for a 'Pratt Senior College.' " 1964. (b)

NYQUIST, E. B. Letter to Hans Simons, August 19, 1957.

NYQUIST, E. B. Letter to Robert F. Wagner, June 3, 1965.

ORTON, D. Interview at New York, N.Y. December 16, 1968.

ORTON, D. "Report of the Principal of Stockton Junior College for the Year Ending June 30, 1956." n.d.

ORVIS, P. B. Letter to Gustave G. Rosenberg, December 20, 1963.

Pacific Weekly (Stockton, Calif.). December 11, 1936, p. 1; November 17, 1950, p. 1.

PATTILLO, M. M., JR., and MACKENZIE, D. M. *Church-Sponsored Higher Education in the United States. Report of the Danforth Commission.* Washington, D.C.: American Council on Education, 1966.

PEIK, W. E. "General Education, the University of Chicago Baccalaureate Degree, and the Liberal Arts College." *The Southern Association Quarterly*, 1942, *6*, 362–374.

Pennsylvania State University. "Confidential Preliminary Working Draft of a Requested Proposal for Establishment of the Olmsted Campus, The Pennsylvania State University, Middletown, Pennsylvania." 1965.

Pennsylvania State University. "Application of the Pennsylvania State University to the Department of Health, Education and Welfare for the Transfer of the North Complex of the Olmsted Air Force Base." 1966.

Pensacola Journal. October 13, 1956; January 20, 1957 (a); April 8, 1957 (b); April 26, 1961 (a); May 20, 1961 (b); May 12, 1962.

Pensacola News. July 18, 1956; July 20, 1957; March 21, 1958; March 23, 1961 (a); April 14, 1961 (b); April 21, 1961 (c); May 12, 1961 (d); June 1, 1962.

Pensacola News-Journal. April 22, 1957.

Pratt Institute. "Minutes of Board of Trustees, October 13, 1964."

Pratt Institute. *Pratt Institute Bulletin, 1966–67.* Brooklyn, N.Y., 1966.

PROCTOR, W. M. *The Six-Four-Four Plan of School Organization in Pasadena, California.* Pasadena, Calif.: Board of Education, 1933.

ROSENBERG, G. G. Letter to Paul B. Orvis, January 8, 1964.

RUDOLPH, F. *The American College and University: A History.* New York: Knopf, 1965.

SALTZMAN, A. W. "Development of the University of Michigan—Dearborn Center." 1968.

SASS, L. D. Memo to Richard Heindel, December 31, 1963.

SCHULTZ, R. E., and STICKLER, H. W. "Vertical Extension of Academic Programs in Institutions of Higher Education." *The Educational Record*, 1965, *46*, 231–241.

SEYMOUR, T. D. "The Three Years' College Course." *The School Review*, 1897, *5*, 709–728.

SIMONS, H. "Further Report on the Day College." 1957. (a) (On file at the New School, New York, N.Y.)

SIMONS, H. Memorandum to the Education Policy Committee, 1957. (b)

SIMONS, H. "Memorandum on the Budget of the New School College." 1958. (a)

SIMONS, H. Memorandum to the Board of Trustees, January 20, 1958. (b)

SIMONS, H. Interview at New York, N.Y. December 16, 1968.

SMART, J. M. *Feasibility and Desirability of Eliminating Lower Division Programs at Selected Campuses of the University of California and the California State Colleges*. Sacramento, Calif.: Coordinating Council for Higher Education, 1967.

STALLWORTH, H. "Analysis of the Anonymous Publication Entitled 'The Case for Conversion of the Pensacola Junior College' (September, 1962)." 1962. (a)

STALLWORTH, H. Letter to John Guy Fowlkes, October 30, 1962. (b)

STALLWORTH, H. Memorandum to J. B. Culpepper, January 23, 1963.

STALLWORTH, H. Letter to Robert A. Altman, December 16, 1968.

State Board of Control of Florida. "Minutes from November 11, 1954 through December 12, 1957."

State Board of Control of Florida. "Official Minutes of the Board of Control, January 16, 1958–June 16, 1961."

State Board of Control of Florida. "A Joint Statement of the Board of Control and the State Junior College Advisory Board Concerning Providing for Higher Education in the West Florida Area." 1963.

State Board of Control of Florida. "Official Minutes of the Board of Control, June 29, 1961–December 4, 1964."

State Board of Education of the Commonwealth of Pennsylvania. "Minutes, 26th Meeting of the State Board of Education." 1965. (a)

State Board of Education of the Commonwealth of Pennsylvania. "Minutes, 27th Meeting of the State Board of Education." 1965. (b)

State Board of Education of the Commonwealth of Pennsylvania. "Minutes, 30th Meeting of the State Board of Education." 1966.

State Board of Regents of Florida. *Planning for a New State Institution of Higher Learning in Dade County, Florida*. Tallahassee, Fla., 1968.

State Junior College Advisory Board of Florida. "Minutes of Meeting, State Junior College Advisory Board, November 15, 1962."

State Junior College Advisory Board of Florida. "Minutes of Meeting, State Junior College Advisory Board, January 17, 1963."

STAUDINGER, H. Memorandum to Hans Simons, November 27, 1957.

STEFANON, S. Letter to Robert A. Altman, January 2, 1969.

STICKLER, H. W. (Ed.) *Experimental Colleges.* Tallahassee, Fla.: Florida State University, 1964.

Stockton (California) Board of Education. "Records of the High School Board, May 5, 1931–June 29, 1937."

Stockton (California) Board of Education. "Records of the Elementary Division, November 12, 1941–January 9, 1945."

Stockton (California) Board of Education. "Board Minutes, January 3, 1949–February 9, 1951."

STORR, R. J. *Harper's University: The Beginnings.* Chicago: University of Chicago Press, 1966.

SWIFT, A. L. "The New School: A Tentative and Confidential Analysis of the New School of Social Research." 1952.

SWIFT, A. L. Memorandum to Hans Simons, November 25, 1957.

TEWKESBURY, D. G. *The Founding of American Colleges and Universities Before the Civil War.* New York: Bureau of Publications, Teachers College, Columbia University, 1932.

TOLLEY, W. P. "A Counterfeit Bachelor's Degree." *The Educational Record,* 1942, *23,* 593–601.

TOTTEN, W. F. Interview at Flint, Mich. April 3, 1968.

TUCKER, W. J. "The Integrity of the College Unit." *The School Review,* 1897, *5,* 683–696.

University of Chicago. *The Departments of Arts, Literature, and Science of The University of Chicago, January, 1895. Circular of Information.* Chicago, 1895.

University of Chicago. *The Departments of Arts, Literature, and Science of The University of Chicago: 1898. Circular of Information.* Chicago, 1898.

University of Chicago. *Arts, Literature and Science for the Sessions of 1931–32.* Chicago, 1931.

University of Michigan. *Proceedings of the Board of Regents, July, 1948–June, 1951.* Ann Arbor, Mich., 1951.

University of Michigan. *Proceedings of the Board of Regents, August, 1951–June, 1954.* Ann Arbor, Mich., 1954.

University of Michigan. "Cooperative Educational Project." 1956. (a)

University of Michigan. Minutes of meeting between representatives of Ford Motor Company and University of Michigan, September 14, 1956. (b)

University of Michigan. Minutes of meeting between representatives of Ford Motor Company and University of Michigan, November 3, 1956. (c)

University of Michigan. "Request for Funds for *University of Michigan—Dearborn Center.*" 1956. (d)

University of Michigan. *Proceedings of the Board of Regents, August, 1954–June, 1957.* Ann Arbor, Mich., 1957.

University of Michigan. "Testimony and Related Material for the State Board of Education." 1965.

University of Michigan. *Proceedings of the Board of Regents, July 26, 1963–June 23, 1966.* Ann Arbor, Mich., 1966.

University of Michigan. "Report of the Dearborn Campus Planning Study Committee." 1969.

University of the State of New York. *Regents Position on Additional Higher Education Facilities on Long Island. A Supplemental Statement on Meeting the Needs in Higher Education in New York State.* Albany: State Education Department, 1957. (a)

University of the State of New York. *Statement and Recommendations by the Board of Regents for Meeting the Needs in Higher Education in New York State, Adopted December 21, 1956.* Albany: State Education Department, 1957. (b)

University of the State of New York. *The Regents Statewide Plan for the Expansion and Development of Higher Education, 1964.* Albany: State Education Department, 1965.

WALKER, E. A. Letter to Edward C. First, Jr., September 8, 1965. (a)

WALKER, E. A. Letter to William W. Scranton, August 24, 1965. (b)

WALKER, E. A. *The Pennsylvania State University and the Commonwealth's Master Plan: An Analysis.* University Park, Pa.: The Pennsylvania State University, 1965. (c)

WALKER, E. A. Letter to Frank N. Hawkins, March 19, 1966. (a)

WALKER, E. A. Letter to Otis G. McCreery, February 23, 1966. (b)

WALKER, E. A. Memorandum to the State Board of Education. 1966. (c) (On file at Pennsylvania State University, University Park, Pa.)

WALKER, E. A. Interview at University Park, Pa. September 18, 1968.

WATTENBARGER, J. Telephone interview. December 9, 1968.

WAYLAND, F. *Report to the Corporation of Brown University on Changes in the System of Collegiate Education, Read March 28, 1850.* Providence, R.I.: George H. Whitney, 1850.

WEST, A. F. "The Length of the Baccalaureate Course and Preparation for the Professional Schools." *Journal of Proceedings and Addresses of the National Education Association,* 1903, 509–514.

WHALEY, R. M. Unpublished chapter from study to be published by the American Council on Education, 1970.

WILBUR, R. L. *Annual Report of the President of Stanford University.* Trustees Series No. 36. Stanford, Calif.: Stanford University, 1920.

WILBUR, R. L. *Annual Report of the President of Stanford University.* Stanford, Calif.: Stanford University, 1927.

WILBUR, R. L. *Annual Report of the President of Stanford University.* Stanford, Calif.: Stanford University, 1928.

WILLIAMS, K. Interview at Boca Raton, Fla. November 14, 1968.

WILLIAMS, K. *The President's Report for the Biennium July 1962 Through June 1964.* Boca Raton, Fla.: Florida Atlantic University, n.d.

WILLIAMSON, A. B. Interview at New York, N.Y. February 26, 1968.

WINTER, C. G. *History of the Junior College Movement in California.* Release No. 20. Sacramento, Calif.: Bureau of Junior College Education, California State Department of Education, 1964.

Name Index

A

ADAMS, C. K., 17
ADAMS, J., 84, 86
ANDERSON, C. H., 100
ANDERSON, J. A., 84, 86, 121, 124
ANGELL, C. N., 13, 15
ASCOLI, M., 48
ASHLER, P., 114, 118
ASHMORE, H., 111, 114
AUSTILL, A., 145, 147, 148, 149

B

BALLENGER, W. S., 87
BARNARD, F. A. P., 17
BATES, G. J., 122, 123, 124, 125

BEARD, C., 47, 52
BLOCH, C. D., 39n
BLOCKER, C., 152
BLOOM, B. S., 77n, 78n
BOUCHER, S., 34n
BOWKER, A. H., 135, 138
BOWLES, F., 142
BRENNAN, T. J., 126
BRICK, M., 35n
BROOKS, R. P., 10
BROWN, S., 31
BROWNELL, R., 122
BRUMBAUGH, A. J., 94, 95, 97, 106, 107, 108, 109, 110, 111
BRYANT, F., 108, 111
BUGAS, J. S., 100, 102
BUNKER, F., 32n

Subject Index

A

Academy for Educational Development, 151n
Adult education, 46, 50, 53, 81, 87, 146
American Association of University Women, 57
American Chemical Society, 73, 74
Arts, Bachelor of, 174, 175; at Brown, 3–4; at Chicago, 56–60, 77–78; as four-year degree, 2–3, 157; at New School, 146; as preparation for graduate school, 18–19; tied to master's degree, 137, 141, 144, 152

B

Associate degree, 59, 174, 175; at Capitol Campus, 152, 155; at Commonwealth Campus, 150
Association of American Colleges, 57
Association of Colleges and Universities of the Pacific Southwest, 57

Bates Committee, 122, 123, 124, 125
Bisection of the baccalaureate, 56, 158; alternatives to, 68; at Chicago, 23; at College of the Pacific, 38–45; at Flint, 88; at Johns Hopkins, 33; at Stanford, 27–29